# New York State

## *May to May Mathematics*

D1400515

Continental

## Acknowledgments

Photo Credits: Front cover, title page, page 17: www.istockphoto.com/SummitView

ISBN 978-0-8454-6962-0

# Table of Contents

# Welcome to New York State May to May Mathematics!

Mathematics is more than numbers. It's more than knowing how to add, subtract, multiply, and divide. You use math when you estimate the distance you ran at soccer practice. You use it when you calculate your chances of winning a game. It helps you interpret a graph in a textbook and use a protractor to measure the angle of a roof.

This book was written to help you get ready for the New York State Mathematics test. Why do you need it? You've been studying math ever since you started school. As you get close to a test, the best way to prepare is to review the ideas and practice the skills you will need for it.

***New York State May to May Mathematics*** contains lessons to review the things you have learned in math class. Each lesson includes examples to show you what the idea means or how the skill is used. On the right side of the lesson page is a sidebar. It contains hints and reminders of things that are related to the main idea of the lesson. After each lesson, there are problems to help you practice what you have reviewed.

The practice pages have several kinds of problems. That's because the real New York State test has more than one kind of question. The problems in this book will help you find out what you know about math ideas, skills, and problem solving. Just as on real math tests, some of the problems in this book are very easy. Others may make you think a bit. And a few will be a challenge.

- The first practice page has **multiple-choice** problems. These problems give you four answers to choose from. In each lesson of this book, the first problem is always a sample. A box under this item tells you how to find the correct answer.

  When you answer a multiple-choice question, be sure to read all the answer choices carefully before choosing one. Some answers can be tricky.

- The next page has **short-response** questions that you must answer in writing. Each one has two parts. In the first part, you usually need to figure out the solution to the problem. You may be asked to show your work. Or you might need to write a short answer or draw a diagram. In the second part, you will have to identify your solution or explain why your answer is correct. You may need to describe the steps you took to find it.

The first short-response problem is a sample. A box under it explains the answer and how to find it. The second problem you must do on your own.

To answer a writing question, follow the item directions *exactly*. Ask yourself, "Am I answering the question that is being asked?" Always think about what you will say *before* writing an explanation. Your thoughts should be clear and organized. Your writing should be neat so it can be read. If you are asked to show your work, be sure the steps are easy to follow and your answer is labeled.

- The last page of practice has an **extended-response** problem. This is the same kind of problem as the short-response items, but it is longer. Often, an extended-response item has three parts. Occasionally it will have only two parts, but each of those parts may call for a little more work than usual. For example, an extended-response question might ask you to make a graph or draw a geometric figure.

At the end of each unit are three pages of review problems. The problems in this section cover all the lessons in that unit, in a mixed order. The review includes all three types of problems you worked with in the lessons: multiple-choice, short-response, and extended-response problems.

A practice test, glossary, and a set of flash cards are at the end of this book. The practice test addresses all the skills you have reviewed. It is set up just like the real New York State test. The glossary lists important terms and their definitions. The flash cards show some of the important math ideas you have reviewed. Cut out the flash cards so you can review these ideas. Practice by yourself or with a friend. There are blank flash cards so you can make some of your own!

# Understanding Mathematical Processes

Learning mathematics has two parts. One part is **mathematical content.** Content includes the skills and ideas you use when you divide numbers, read the degree marks on a protractor, recognize similar figures, interpret data on a line graph, or calculate the perimeter of a backyard.

Another equally important part is **mathematical processes.** These are the skills you use to help you understand and apply the ideas in the content areas. You use them when you explain these ideas to others. And you especially use them when you solve problems.

There are many process skills, and they often overlap. Process skills include:

- **Representation**
- **Connections**
- **Communication**
- **Reasoning and Proof**
- **Problem Solving**

All of these process skills are important in helping you to master mathematical content. They are tied together with content skills—you can't really learn them separately. As you work through a math problem, you may use several process and content skills. This is especially true when you are answering an open-ended question like a short- or extended-response problem.

For example, suppose you are asked to solve a word problem and explain why your answer is correct. You use a problem-solving strategy to figure out the answer. If you write a number sentence to show the mathematics of the word problem, you are using representation. To justify your answer, you use reasoning and proof skills. If you mention a general mathematical rule to prove your answer, you are showing connections. And the written explanation, using the appropriate mathematics vocabulary, demonstrates your communication skills.

The problems in this book are just like those on the actual test. So you will practice both content skills and process skills as you work through the lessons in this book.

In the following sections, you'll see some examples of the kinds of problems that use these process skills.

### Representation

Representation problems may ask you to create a model to show a mathematical idea or to organize and record information. Or you might have to choose the correct representation or explain what a model means. These representations can take many forms: pictures, diagrams, models, tallies, graphs, geometric figures, expressions and equations, patterns, and more.

Here's an example of a problem that calls for representation skills.

Mark and label the fraction $\frac{3}{10}$ on the number line.

This problem asks you to show where the fraction $\frac{3}{10}$ is located on a number line. The number line has ten equal sections from 0 to 1. So each tick mark stands for $\frac{1}{10}$. To find $\frac{3}{10}$, count over three tick marks from 0. Draw a dot on the third tick mark and label $\frac{3}{10}$ above it.

### Connections

Connections problems may ask you to recognize how mathematical ideas are related or build on each other. Or you may need to use a related idea to solve a problem. Sometimes you need to apply a mathematical connection to a real-life situation. You may need to show how mathematics is part of everyday life.

Here's an example of a problem that calls for connections skills.

What value of $a$ makes this equation true?

$$7 \times a = 42$$

This problem asks you to find the value of $a$ in a multiplication problem. You may remember that multiplication and division are related. They are inverse, or opposite, operations. So you can use this connection to solve the problem. You think:

*"7 times some number is 42. That's the same as 42 divided by 7...6."*

## Communication

Mathematical ideas are most useful when they can be shared. Problems that practice your communication skills may ask you to explain how you solved a problem or why an answer is correct. You may be asked to express a mathematical idea, using the words and phrases that make up mathematical language. To do well on these problems, you should be able to organize your thoughts clearly. You should also know the meanings of mathematical words so you can use them correctly.

Here's an example of a problem that calls for communication skills.

Two triangles are similar. What must be true about them?

To answer this question, you must know the meaning of the word *similar*. You will have learned this term when you studied geometric figures. You might write a response like this:

A triangle is a figure with three sides and three angles. Similar figures have the same shape but may be different sizes. So similar triangles will be identical in shape but can be different sizes.

## Reasoning and Proof

Understanding *why* is just as important as understanding *how* in mathematics. Problems that focus on reasoning skills may ask you to prove that a mathematical statement is true or false. To do this, you should be able to think logically about the idea and to provide examples to justify your argument. Often you will rely on mathematical connections to support your thoughts. Understanding and using mathematical vocabulary correctly also matters. Here again, organizing your thoughts is important. A proof is easiest to understand when it leads from one step to the next.

Here's an example of a problem that calls for reasoning and proof skills.

What is the measure of the missing angle? Explain how you found your answer.

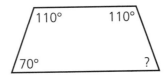

This problem asks you to find the measure of the missing angle of a trapezoid. Three of the angle measures are given. You may remember that the sum of the interior angles of a quadrilateral is 360°, so you can add the given measures and subtract to find the measure of the fourth angle. You might write something like this:

> The measure of all four angles of a trapezoid is 360°. Add to find the measure of the given angles: 110° + 110° + 70° = 290°. Then subtract the total measure of the three angles from 360°: 360° − 290° = 70°. The measure of the missing angle is 70°.

## Problem Solving

Some mathematics problems test your understanding of mathematical ideas. Others test your skills in computation or other procedures. But many problems call for more than just recalling a fact or doing a calculation. They require you to analyze a situation and figure out a way to find an answer. They may be word problems, but they can be other types of problems, like geometry, too. You need to be able to put your different skills together to solve a problem.

You should know and be able to use the **four-step problem-solving procedure.**

1. **Read** the problem. What is the question? What kind of information does the problem give? To be sure you understand the problem, you can restate it in your own words.

2. **Plan** how to find a solution. What steps must you take? What calculations must you make? Does the problem have all the information you need or is something missing? Is there information in the problem that is not needed and that you can ignore? What strategy will you use? To develop a plan, identify the steps you must take to solve the problem.

3. **Solve** the problem. Do you need to show your work? Be careful to carry out your plan in a clear, step-by-step fashion. Ask yourself if someone else could follow your steps.

4. **Check** your answer. Does it make sense? Think about your answer in light of the question that was asked. If the answer does not make sense, go back and try again.

Mathematical Processes

You should also know and be able to use a variety of **problem-solving strategies.** Some strategies you should be familiar with are listed here.

- Guess and check
- Draw a picture or diagram
- Look for a pattern
- Reason it out
- Make a table or a list
- Work backward
- Break it into steps
- Write a number sentence
- Work a simpler problem

Here's an example of a word problem test item that calls for problem-solving skills.

Josef has a total of 35 yards of wire to put up a fence. He used 9 yards of wire for the first side of the fence and 10.5 yards for the second side. How much wire is left for the third and fourth sides of the fence? Show your work.

To solve this problem, read it carefully and make a plan for solving it. First you need to find the amount of wire used for sides one and two, which calls for addition. Then you need to find the amount of wire left for sides three and four by subtracting the total from 35 yards. Once you have your plan, carry out your work and check it. Your response might look like this.

$$
\begin{array}{r}
9.0 \\
+10.5 \\
\hline
19.5
\end{array}
\qquad
\begin{array}{r}
35.0 \\
-19.5 \\
\hline
15.5
\end{array}
$$

There will be 15.5 yards of wire left for sides three and four of the fence.

Many problems require not only the problem-solving skills, but all the process skills—reasoning, connections, representation, and communication. You'll be using all of these skills in this book as you work through the lessons and practice problems in each of the content strands.

# Unit 1
## Whole Numbers and Fractions

You use numbers every day. You may count the number of times you can jump rope without stopping. You may write a number to guess how many pennies are in a jar. There is a number on the back of your soccer jersey. There are numbers that name highways. Not all numbers are whole numbers. Fractions describe parts of a whole. You can use fractions to show the amount of pizza you ate. You could describe how many puppies in a group are black with a fraction. You use whole numbers and fractions in all areas of math. This unit will help you understand whole numbers and fractions.

Lesson 1 **Place Value and Whole Numbers** reviews how to read and write whole numbers in different ways. You will also find the value of different places in a number.

Lesson 2 **Equivalent Fractions** reviews how to name a fraction in higher and lower terms.

Lesson 3 **Comparing and Ordering Fractions** reviews how to put fractions in order from least to greatest or greatest to least. You will also use the > and < symbols to compare fractions.

# Place Value and Whole Numbers

**Indicators**   5.N.1, 2, 3   **CCSS**   5.NBT.1

✓ Numbers may be expressed in various ways.

- **word form**

  four million, one hundred thirty-seven thousand,
  two hundred eighty-two

- **standard form**

  4,137,282

- **expanded form**

  4,000,000 + 100,000 + 30,000 + 7,000 + 200 + 80 + 2

✓ The **place value** of a digit depends on its position in a number.

| MILLIONS | HUNDRED THOUSANDS | TEN THOUSANDS | THOUSANDS | HUNDREDS | TENS | ONES |
|---|---|---|---|---|---|---|
| 4, | 1 | 3 | 7, | 2 | 8 | 2 |

What is the value of the 4 in 4,137,282?
The 4 is in the millions place, so it is 4,000,000.

✓ You can **compare** numbers by looking at the digits in the same places.

Which number is greater, 873,615 or 837,165?

Line up the numbers. Starting at the highest place value, find where they differ.

873,615
837,165

These numbers first differ in the ten-thousands place. The 7 is greater than the 3, so 873,615 > 837,165.

## Remember—

Numbers may be expressed in model form.

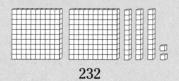
232

The symbol > means "is greater than." The symbol < means "is less than." The symbol *always* points to the smaller number.

49 < 94
94 > 49

The value of each place is 10 times the value of the place to the right.

The 5 in **5**87 is ten times greater (500) than the 5 in 8**5**7 (50).

10 ones = 1 ten

10 tens = 1 hundred

10 hundreds = 1 thousand

10 thousands = 1 ten thousand

10 ten thousands = 1 hundred thousand

10 hundred thousands = 1 million

**Read each problem. Circle the letter of the best answer.**

**1** Which of these numbers is the same as 80,000 + 40 + 5?

   **A** 80,450      **C** 84,050

   **B** 80,045      **D** 840,005

The correct answer is B. When the digits are added up, they total 80,045. Choice A would be written in expanded form as 80,000 + 400 + 50. Choice C would be written as 80,000 + 4,000 + 50. Choice D is equivalent to 800,000 + 40,000 + 5.

**2** Monique wants to use the digits 4, 1, 9, and 8 to make the largest possible number. What number will Monique make?

   **A** 9,814      **C** 8,941

   **B** 9,418      **D** 9,841

**3** Carlos started with the number 37,068. What is the largest increase possible by replacing one of the digits with a 4?

   **A** 40      **C** 4,000

   **B** 100      **D** 10,000

**4** Which is the same as 631,051?

   **A** six hundred thirty-one thousand, fifty-one

   **B** six hundred thirteen thousand, five hundred one

   **C** six hundred thirty-one thousand, five hundred ten

   **D** sixty-three thousand, fifty-one

**5** In which number does the 6 have the smallest value?

   **A** 1,784,635      **C** 1,746,835

   **B** 1,674,358      **D** 1,467,583

**6** New York State covers an area of about 141,090 square kilometers. Which of the following is the same as this number?

   **A** 100,000 + 400 + 90

   **B** 100,000 + 4,000 + 100 + 90

   **C** 100,000 + 40,000 + 100 + 90

   **D** 100,000 + 40,000 + 1,000 + 90

**7** The number line shows the number of students in four schools.

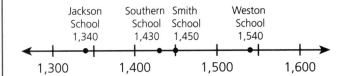

If the number of students attending Jackson School increased by 200, which statement would be true?

   **A** Jackson School and Weston School would have the same number of students.

   **B** Weston School would have the most students.

   **C** Smith School would have the fewest students.

   **D** Jackson School would have the second most students.

**Read each problem. Write your answers.**

**8** In 2009, the average income of a four-person family in New York State was $83,036.

**Part A**

If the ones and thousands digits were switched, what would the average income be?

*Answer:* $ _86,033_

**Part B**

Explain your answer.

> In the original number, there is a 6 in the ones place and a 3 in the thousands place. If these digits are switched, there would be a 3 in the ones place and a 6 in the thousands place.

**9** Jocelyn wrote two 5-digit numbers. There were only 2's and 3's used as digits. The first number had a 2 in the ten-thousands, thousands, and tens places. The second number had a 2 in the ten-thousands, hundreds, and ones places.

**Part A**

What are the two numbers that Jocelyn wrote?

*Answer:* _____ and _____

**Part B**

Plot and label the two numbers on the number line below.

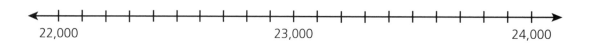

22,000          23,000          24,000

**Unit 1** Whole Numbers and Fractions

**Read the problem. Write your answer for each part.**

**10** In 1907, 285,731 people immigrated to the United States from Italy. Most of them passed through Ellis Island.

**Part A**

How would that number of people be written in word form?

*Answer:* _____

_____

> *Ask Yourself*
> What are the three ways to express the same number?

**Part B**

Write the number in expanded form.

*Answer:* _____

**Part C**

The same year, the number of immigrants arriving from Russia, expressed in expanded form, was 200,000 + 50,000 + 8,000 + 900 + 40 + 3. How is this number written in standard form?

*Answer:* _____

# Equivalent Fractions

**Indicator 5.N.4**

✅ A **fraction** can name part of a whole or part of a set.

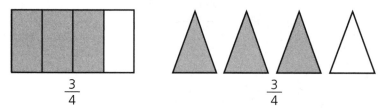

$$\frac{3}{4}$$          $$\frac{3}{4}$$

✅ Fractions can be shown on a **number line.**

This number line shows halves, thirds, fourths, and sixths.

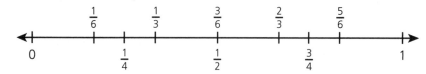

✅ **Equivalent fractions** name the same number in different terms.

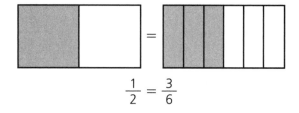

$$\frac{1}{2} = \frac{3}{6}$$

The fractions $\frac{1}{2}$ and $\frac{3}{6}$ are equivalent.

To find an equivalent fraction in **higher terms,** multiply the numerator and the denominator by the same number.

$$\frac{1}{2} \times \frac{3}{3} = \frac{1 \times 3}{2 \times 3} = \frac{3}{6}$$

To find an equivalent fraction in lower terms, divide the numerator and the denominator by the same number.

$$\frac{3}{6} \div \frac{3}{3} = \frac{3 \div 3}{6 \div 3} = \frac{1}{2}$$

---

*Remember—*

The **numerator** and **denominator** are the **terms** of the fraction.

$$\frac{2}{6} \begin{array}{l} \leftarrow \text{Numerator} \\ \leftarrow \text{Denominator} \end{array}$$

The numerator is the number of parts being talked about. The denominator is the number of parts in the whole or set.

When a fraction is in **lowest terms,** or simplest form, it cannot be made simpler.

$$\frac{2}{6} = \frac{1}{3}$$

---

**Unit 1** Whole Numbers and Fractions

**Read each problem. Circle the letter of the best answer.**

**1** Joan walked $\frac{3}{5}$ mile. Which fraction is equivalent to $\frac{3}{5}$ in higher terms?

  **A** $\frac{3}{10}$       **C** $\frac{9}{20}$

  **B** $\frac{6}{10}$       **D** $\frac{15}{20}$

> The correct answer is B. Three-fifths is equivalent to six-tenths when the numerator and denominator are each multiplied by 2. Choices A, C, and D are not equivalent.

**2** Lily used $\frac{18}{20}$ of a bag of raisins to make trail mix. What fraction is equivalent to $\frac{18}{20}$?

  **A** $\frac{8}{20}$       **C** $\frac{9}{10}$

  **B** $\frac{8}{10}$       **D** $\frac{4}{5}$

**3** Look at this figure. Which of these numbers does **not** name the shaded part of this figure?

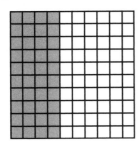

  **A** $\frac{40}{100}$       **C** $\frac{2}{5}$

  **B** $\frac{10}{20}$       **D** $\frac{8}{20}$

**4** Forty of every sixty homes in a town were painted white. Which fraction is equivalent to $\frac{40}{60}$?

  **A** $\frac{1}{2}$       **C** $\frac{3}{4}$

  **B** $\frac{2}{3}$       **D** $\frac{3}{5}$

**5** What is an equivalent fraction for $\frac{7}{21}$?

  **A** $\frac{1}{7}$       **C** $\frac{3}{7}$

  **B** $\frac{3}{21}$       **D** $\frac{1}{3}$

**6** About $\frac{1}{4}$ of all people living in New York are under 18 years old. How can an equivalent fraction be found for $\frac{1}{4}$?

  **A** divide 1 and 4 by 2

  **B** multiply 1 by 2 and 4 by 4

  **C** multiply 1 and 4 by 2

  **D** divide 1 by 4 and 4 by 1

**7** Which fraction is equivalent to $\frac{1}{6}$?

  **A** $\frac{4}{24}$

  **B** $\frac{4}{28}$

  **C** $\frac{6}{24}$

  **D** $\frac{5}{35}$

**Read each problem. Write your answers.**

**8** The figure at the right shows the fraction $\frac{6}{30}$.

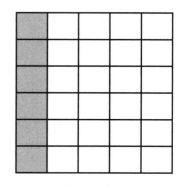

**Part A**

What is an equivalent fraction in lowest terms?

*Show your work.*

$$\frac{6}{30} = \frac{6 \div 6}{30 \div 6} = \frac{1}{5}$$

Answer: _____ $\frac{1}{5}$ _____

**Part B**

What is an equivalent fraction in higher terms?

Answer: _____ $\frac{12}{60}$ _____

> To find an equivalent fraction in lowest terms, divide the numerator and the denominator by the greatest common factor of 6 and 30: 6. So $\frac{6}{30} \div \frac{6}{6} = \frac{1}{5}$. To change a fraction to higher terms, multiply the numerator and denominator by the same number. You can multiply both 6 and 30 by 2. In higher terms, $\frac{6}{30}$ is $\frac{12}{60}$.

**9** Parker had a tablet of 50 sheets of paper. He used 20 sheets to design Nature Club fliers.

**Part A**

What fraction of the tablet did Parker use? Write the fraction in lowest terms.

Answer: _____

**Part B**

Parker used 60 notecards from a pack of 150. Is the fraction of notecards Parker used the same as the fraction in Part A? Tell why or why not.

_____

_____

_____

**Read the problem. Write your answer for each part.**

10  During the Civil War, about $\frac{3}{10}$ of all soldiers in the Union Army came from New York State.

### Part A

What is an equivalent fraction that represents the same fraction as $\frac{3}{10}$ in higher terms?

*Show your work.*

**Ask Yourself**
Do I multiply or divide the numerator and denominator to find a fraction in higher terms?

*Answer:* _____

### Part B

Can you write $\frac{3}{10}$ in lowest terms? Explain why or why not.

_____

_____

_____

_____

**Indicators  5.N.5, 9**

✓ To compare fractions, first find equivalent fractions with the same denominators. Then compare the numerators.

Estelle had two packages of nuts. One weighed $\frac{3}{5}$ pound and the other weighed $\frac{1}{2}$ pound. Which package weighed more?

First change the fractions to equivalent fractions with a denominator of 10.

$$\frac{3}{5} \times \frac{2}{2} = \frac{3 \times 2}{5 \times 2} = \frac{6}{10} \qquad \frac{1}{2} \times \frac{5}{5} = \frac{1 \times 5}{2 \times 5} = \frac{5}{10}$$

Now compare the numerators of the equivalent fractions.

$$\frac{6}{10} > \frac{5}{10}$$

The package weighing $\frac{3}{5}$ pound weighs more.

✓ To compare fractions with different denominators, you can use a number line.

Cory ran $\frac{1}{3}$ mile. Stacey ran $\frac{1}{4}$ mile. Who ran a farther distance?

Find $\frac{1}{3}$ and $\frac{1}{4}$ on a number line.

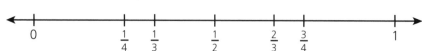

The fraction $\frac{1}{3}$ is to the right of $\frac{1}{4}$, so it is the larger fraction. Cory ran a farther distance.

*Remember—*

Different fractions with the same denominator have **common denominators.** To compare fractions, always find equivalent fractions with common denominators.

To find a common denominator, find a third number that is a factor of both numbers. For example, 3 and 4 are both factors of 12, so 12 is a common denominator of 3 and 4.

The symbol $>$ means "is greater than."

$$\frac{4}{12} > \frac{3}{12}$$

The symbol $<$ means "is less than."

$$\frac{3}{12} < \frac{4}{12}$$

The symbol *always* points toward the smaller number.

To **order** fractions, first compare them. Then put them in order from least to greatest or greatest to least.

**Unit 1** Whole Numbers and Fractions

**Read each problem. Circle the letter of the best answer.**

**1** Look at these fractions.

$$\frac{3}{4} \qquad \frac{4}{6} \qquad \frac{5}{8}$$

Which list shows the fractions in order from smallest to largest?

**A** $\frac{3}{4}, \frac{5}{8}, \frac{4}{6}$

**B** $\frac{4}{6}, \frac{3}{4}, \frac{5}{8}$

**C** $\frac{5}{8}, \frac{4}{6}, \frac{3}{4}$

**D** $\frac{3}{4}, \frac{4}{6}, \frac{5}{8}$

The correct answer is C. The common denominator for these fractions is 24: $\frac{3}{4} = \frac{18}{24}, \frac{4}{6} = \frac{16}{24}, \frac{5}{8} = \frac{15}{24}$. Then compare: $\frac{15}{24} < \frac{16}{24} < \frac{18}{24}$.

**2** Which of these fractions is the smallest?

**A** $\frac{1}{4}$        **C** $\frac{1}{8}$

**B** $\frac{1}{2}$        **D** $\frac{3}{16}$

**3** A hot chocolate recipe uses $\frac{1}{2}$ cup of cocoa, $\frac{7}{8}$ cup of milk, and $\frac{1}{4}$ cup of sugar for each serving. Which list shows the amounts of ingredients from least to greatest?

**A** sugar, cocoa, milk

**B** milk, sugar, cocoa

**C** sugar, milk, cocoa

**D** milk, cocoa, sugar

**4** The table shows the fraction of students in each class who wore a team jersey to school.

| Class | Students Who Wore a Team Jersey |
|-------|-------------------------------|
| 101 | $\frac{2}{9}$ |
| 102 | $\frac{1}{3}$ |
| 103 | $\frac{5}{18}$ |
| 104 | $\frac{10}{27}$ |

Which lists the classes from the smallest fraction to the largest?

**A** 102, 104, 103, 101

**B** 101, 103, 102, 104

**C** 101, 103, 104, 102

**D** 104, 102, 103, 101

**5** Which of the following is true?

**A** $\frac{5}{6} < \frac{3}{4}$      **C** $\frac{1}{2} < \frac{3}{4}$

**B** $\frac{1}{2} > \frac{5}{8}$      **D** $\frac{3}{4} = \frac{7}{8}$

**6** Jamecia walked $\frac{3}{5}$ mile. Jason walked a shorter distance than Jamecia did. Which could be the distance Jason walked?

**A** $\frac{2}{10}$ mile      **C** $\frac{15}{20}$ mile

**B** $\frac{25}{40}$ mile      **D** $\frac{3}{4}$ mile

**7** Which of these fractions is the largest?

**A** $\frac{2}{3}$      **C** $\frac{5}{12}$

**B** $\frac{2}{4}$      **D** $\frac{7}{24}$

**Read each problem. Write your answers.**

**8** The table shows the weights of three tomatoes from Danielle's garden.

| Tomato | Weight (in pounds) |
|--------|--------------------|
| 1 | $\frac{11}{16}$ |
| 2 | $\frac{3}{4}$ |
| 3 | $\frac{5}{8}$ |

*Part A*

Write the weights of the tomatoes in order from lightest to heaviest.

*Answer:* _____ $\frac{5}{8}, \frac{11}{16}, \frac{3}{4}$ _____ pound

*Part B*

Explain why your answer is correct.

To compare these fractions, first change them to equivalent fractions with a common denominator. These fractions have a common denominator of 16: $\frac{3}{4} = \frac{12}{16}$ and $\frac{5}{8} = \frac{10}{16}$. Then compare the fractions: $\frac{10}{16} < \frac{11}{16} < \frac{12}{16}$. So $\frac{5}{8} < \frac{11}{16} < \frac{3}{4}$.

**9** The highest peak in the Catskill Mountains is Slide Mountain.

*Part A*

Juan, Danica, and Trevor decided to walk to the top of Slide Mountain, but they didn't make it all the way. Juan hiked $\frac{2}{3}$ of the way, Danica hiked $\frac{3}{4}$ of the way, and Trevor made it $\frac{7}{12}$ of the way. Using < or >, show the distances completed from greatest to least.

*Answer:* _____

*Part B*

A fourth friend, Marcus, hiked $\frac{3}{5}$ of the way up Slide Mountain. How could you compare the distance he hiked with the others?

_____

_____

**Unit 1** Whole Numbers and Fractions

**Read the problem. Write your answer for each part.**

10 Niagara Falls, on the border between the United States and Canada, consists of two falls, the Horseshoe Falls and the American Falls.

### Part A

The American Falls plunges 180 feet over a ledge that is about $\frac{2}{3}$ mile wide. Write a fraction that is larger than $\frac{2}{3}$.

Answer: _____

### Part B

There are many ways to see the Falls. The *Maid of the Mist* is a sightseeing boat that travels on a $\frac{1}{2}$-hour trip to the base of the Falls. The Whirlpool Aero Car flies above the Falls. This ride takes about $\frac{1}{6}$ hour. Which trip takes longer?

***Ask Yourself***
What is a common denominator of the fractions?

Answer: _____

Explain how you know.

_____

_____

### Part C

Mark and label $\frac{2}{3}$, $\frac{1}{6}$, and $\frac{1}{2}$ on the number line below.

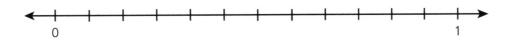

**Read each problem. Circle the letter of the best answer.**

**1** What is $1,000,000 + 60,000 + 80 + 5$ in standard form?

   **A** 1,600,805

   **B** 1,060,850

   **C** 1,600,085

   **D** 1,060,085

**2** Attendance at the food show at the Javits Center was 25,967. Which digit is in the hundreds place?

   **A** 7          **C** 9

   **B** 6          **D** 5

**3** The population of New York State during the last census was 19,378,102. If the digit in the tens place was replaced by a 6, how many more people would be living in New York State?

   **A** 6          **C** 600

   **B** 60         **D** 6,000

**4** Which of the following is equivalent to $\frac{9}{63}$ in lowest terms?

   **A** $\frac{1}{6}$          **C** $\frac{3}{21}$

   **B** $\frac{1}{7}$          **D** $\frac{3}{12}$

**5** Which of these numbers is largest?

   **A** 1,708,365          **C** 1,870,653

   **B** 1,870,365          **D** 1,087,365

**6** A paper clip measures $\frac{3}{4}$ inch long. What fraction is equivalent to $\frac{3}{4}$?

   **A** $\frac{1}{4}$          **C** $\frac{4}{8}$

   **B** $\frac{2}{4}$          **D** $\frac{6}{8}$

**7** Which of the following statements is **not** true?

   **A** $\frac{6}{9} > \frac{5}{8}$          **C** $\frac{2}{3} < \frac{3}{4}$

   **B** $\frac{1}{2} = \frac{6}{12}$          **D** $\frac{3}{4} < \frac{5}{8}$

**8** Look at these fractions.

$$\frac{3}{4} \qquad \frac{3}{5} \qquad \frac{1}{2}$$

Which list shows the fractions in order from largest to smallest?

   **A** $\frac{3}{4}, \frac{3}{5}, \frac{1}{2}$          **C** $\frac{1}{2}, \frac{3}{4}, \frac{3}{5}$

   **B** $\frac{3}{5}, \frac{3}{4}, \frac{1}{2}$          **D** $\frac{3}{5}, \frac{1}{2}, \frac{3}{4}$

**Unit 1** Whole Numbers and Fractions

**Read each problem. Write your answers.**

9   The table shows the populations of four states in 2010.

| State | Population |
|---|---|
| Connecticut | 3,574,097 |
| Kentucky | 4,339,367 |
| Oklahoma | 3,751,351 |
| South Carolina | 4,625,364 |

**Part A**

Order these states from least to greatest population.

Answer: _____

_____

**Part B**

Explain how you found your answer.

_____

_____

_____

10   The figure at the right shows the fraction $\frac{12}{20}$.

Write an equivalent fraction in lowest terms.

**Show your work.**

Answer: _____

11   The distance from the center of the moon to the center of Earth is about 238,700 miles.

**Part A**

Write this number in expanded form.

Answer: _____

**Part B**

Write this number in word form.

Answer: _____

**Read the problem. Write your answer for each part.**

**12** Before the American Revolution in 1776, people came from all over the world to settle in the British colonies. About $\frac{1}{2}$ of the immigrants came from England. The table below shows some of the other places people came from.

| Place of Origin | Fraction of Immigrants |
|---|---|
| Spain | $\frac{2}{50}$ |
| Scotland | $\frac{3}{50}$ |
| Ireland | $\frac{1}{25}$ |
| Africa | $\frac{1}{5}$ |

### Part A

Which two places of origin represented the same fraction of the population?

*Answer:* _____ and _____

### Part B

After England, what was the place that the largest group of immigrants came from?

*Answer:* _____

### Part C

On the lines below, explain how you know your answer is correct.

_____

_____

_____

_____

# Unit 2
## Decimals and Percents

You see decimals and percents every day. In a grocery store, the weights of food are given as decimal numbers. You might buy 3.6 pounds of grapes or a box of cereal that contains 15.2 ounces. Your teacher might use percents to show your grade on a test. You may have scored an 88% on your last spelling test. You can write a percent as a decimal and as a fraction. A ratio is a way to compare two numbers. You might use a ratio to talk about a group of similar things, like the ratio of boys to girls in your class. This unit will help you understand decimals, percents, and ratios.

**Lesson 1** **Decimals** reviews how to read and write decimal numbers. You will also compare and order decimals.

**Lesson 2** **Percents** reviews what a percent is and how to rewrite a percent as a fraction or a decimal. You will also change fractions and decimals to percents.

**Lesson 3** **Ratios** reviews how to write a ratio in different ways. You will also express ratios in lowest terms.

# Decimals

**Indicators** 5.N.8, 10 **CCSS** 5.NBT.3.a, b

✓ A **decimal** names a fractional number in place-value form. Decimal places are written to the right of a decimal point.

A tank held 63.524 gallons of water. What is the word name for this number?

Put the digits in a place-value chart to help you read them.

Read this number as "sixty-three and five hundred twenty-four thousandths."

| TENS | ONES | DECIMAL POINT | TENTHS | HUNDREDTHS | THOUSANDTHS |
|------|------|---------------|--------|------------|-------------|
| 6 | 3 | . | 5 | 2 | 4 |

✓ To compare decimals, compare the digits in the same places.

Which is greater, 1.369 or 1.396?

Look at the digits in the same places, from left to right. The digits in the ones places are the same, 1. The digits in the tenths places are also the same, 3. Next, look at the hundredths place.

1.3**6**9          1.3**9**6

The hundredths digits are different: 9 hundredths is greater than 6 hundredths. So 1.396 > 1.369.

✓ A number line can be used to compare and order decimals.

Which is greater—9.43 or 9.34?

The number line shows that 9.43 is to the right of 9.34. So 9.43 is greater than 9.34.

9.43 > 9.34

---

*Remember—*

You can write decimals in many forms.

• word form
  sixty-one hundredths

• standard form
  0.61

• expanded form
  0.6 + 0.01

The value of each place is 10 times larger than the place to its right.

1 one = 10 tenths
1 tenth = 10 hundredths
1 hundredth =
10 thousandths

Each place value is $\frac{1}{10}$ as large as the place to its left.

Read the decimal point as *and*.

You can write zeros for placeholders. The value of the decimal does not change.

Is 0.2 or 0.09 larger?
0.2 = 0.20, so 0.20 > 0.09.

Numbers to the right of a number line are *always* greater than numbers to the left.

The symbol > means "is greater than."

0.5 > 0.05

The symbol < means "is less than."

0.3 < 3.0

---

**Read each problem. Circle the letter of the best answer.**

**1** What is the word form of 3.419?

 A three and four hundred nineteen

 B three and four hundred nineteen tenths

 C three and four hundred nineteen hundredths

 D three and four hundred nineteen thousandths

> The correct answer is D. This number has a 4 in the tenths place, a 1 in the hundredths place, and a 9 in the thousandths place. The 3 is a whole number, and the decimal point is read as *and*. So the number is *three and four hundred nineteen thousandths*.

**2** Which of these decimals is the smallest?

 A 0.73          C 0.730

 B 0.703          D 0.733

**3** Tiara had a fever of one hundred and nine-tenths degrees. Which of these is the same as one hundred and nine-tenths degrees?

 A 100.09°          C 100.9°

 B 100.99°          D 100.009°

**4** Which of the following choices is true?

 A 0.432 > 0.423

 B 0.671 < 0.617

 C 0.397 < 0.379

 D 0.423 > 0.432

**5** A car was traveling at an average speed of fifty-eight and two-tenths miles per hour. Which of these choices does *not* represent the same speed?

 A 58.200

 B 58.2

 C 58.02

 D 58.20

**6** Mauricio wants to buy his mother a birthday gift. The table below shows his choices.

| Item | Price |
|---|---|
| CD | $15.39 |
| Book | $13.95 |
| Pen Set | $15.93 |
| Mugs | $13.59 |

Which item has the second greatest cost?

 A the CD

 B the pen set

 C the mugs

 D the book

**7** Which of these lists is ordered from least to greatest?

 A 0.8, 0.61, 0.681, 0.16

 B 0.16, 0.681, 0.61, 0.8

 C 0.16, 0.61, 0.681, 0.8

 D 0.61, 0.16, 0.681, 0.8

**Read each problem. Write your answers.**

**8** Angelina wrote two different numbers less than 1 with three digits to the right of the decimal point. Each has a 5 in the tenths place and a 3 in the thousandths place.

**Part A**

Write two decimal numbers that could be the numbers Angelina wrote.

Answer: ___0.583___ and ___0.573___

**Part B**

Describe the steps you would take to compare these two decimals.

> Both numbers have a 5 in the tenths place and a 3 in the thousandths place. Any number can be used for the hundredths place. In this case, 8 and 7 were used. To compare the numbers, line them up vertically. Starting from the left, compare the tenths and then the hundredths places. Then compare the numbers: 0.583 > 0.573.

**9** The police investigated a traffic accident. The tire marks on the road measured 36.207 meters long.

**Part A**

What is the word form of this number?

Answer: _____

**Part B**

What digit is in the hundredths place of this number?

Answer: _____

**Read the problem. Write your answer for each part.**

10  Donovan made this table to show the rainfall received in some cities in New York State one day.

| City | Rainfall (in inches) |
|------|------|
| Elmira | 0.09 |
| Suffern | 0.21 |
| Athens | 0.149 |
| Poughkeepsie | 0.1 |
| Syracuse | 0.15 |

### Part A

How much rain did Suffern receive? Write the word form of the number.

*Answer:* _____ inch

### Part B

Write the amounts of rainfall in order from greatest to least.

*Answer:* _____

*Ask Yourself*
What place value do I look at first?

### Part C

Later, Donovan decided to add a new city name that received the second highest rainfall amount. What could have been the amount of rainfall received?

*Answer:* _____ inch

Explain your answer.

_____

_____

_____

# Percents

**Indicator 5.N.11**

✓ A **percent** names part of a hundred.

About 47% of the students at Central Elementary School are girls.

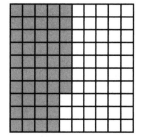

That means that 47 of every 100 students are girls.

47 of 100 = 47% = 0.47

✓ To change a percent to a decimal, drop the percent sign, %, and move the decimal point two places to the **left.**

63% = 0.63          25% = 0.25          9% = 0.09

✓ To change a decimal to a percent, move the decimal point two places to the **right** and add the percent sign.

0.91 = 91%          0.352 = 35.2%          0.04 = 4%

✓ To change a percent to a fraction, drop the percent sign and put the number over 100. Then reduce to lowest terms.

$40\% = \frac{40}{100} = \frac{2}{5}$          $12\% = \frac{12}{100} = \frac{6}{50} = \frac{3}{25}$

---

*Remember—*

You can name the same number as a fraction, a decimal, or a percent.

Fraction: $\frac{53}{100}$

Decimal: 0.53

Percent: 53%

These answers are **equivalent.** They name the same number in different terms.

When a percent is less than 10%, you need to write zeros in order to move the decimal point two places to the left.

3% → **0.03** → 0.03

Here are some common percents you should know:

$10\% = \frac{1}{10} = 0.1$

$25\% = \frac{1}{4} = 0.25$

$50\% = \frac{1}{2} = 0.5$

$75\% = \frac{3}{4} = 0.75$

**Unit 2** Decimals and Percents

**Read each problem. Circle the letter of the best answer.**

**1** What is 50% expressed as a fraction?

A $\frac{1}{50}$   C $\frac{1}{5}$

B $\frac{1}{4}$   D $\frac{1}{2}$

The correct answer is D. A percent is part of a hundred, so rewrite 50% as a fraction with a denominator of 100: $\frac{50}{100}$. Then reduce $\frac{50}{100}$ to lowest terms: $\frac{1}{2}$.

**2** What is 82% expressed as a decimal?

A 8.2   C 0.082

B 0.82   D 8.28

**3** A survey was taken to find the favorite month of a group of students. The results are shown below.

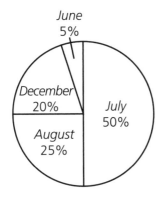

Which month was chosen by $\frac{1}{4}$ of the students?

A August

B December

C July

D June

**4** Which of these numbers does **not** name the shaded part of the figure below?

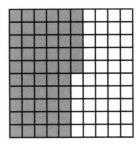

A 55%   C $\frac{11}{20}$

B 0.55   D $\frac{5}{100}$

**5** How is 35% written as a decimal and a fraction?

A 0.35 and $\frac{8}{25}$   C 0.35 and $\frac{7}{20}$

B 3.5 and $\frac{3}{5}$   D 0.035 and $\frac{7}{20}$

**6** What percent does the shaded part show?

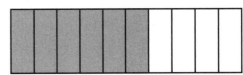

A 6%   C 40%

B 60%   D 4%

**7** The estimated cost of the state capitol building in Albany was 16% of the final cost. Which of these fractions is equivalent to 16%?

A $\frac{5}{20}$   C $\frac{5}{25}$

B $\frac{16}{50}$   D $\frac{4}{25}$

**Read each problem. Write your answers.**

8  On a recent Saturday, 65% of all shoppers in a mall stopped at the food court for something to eat.

*Part A*

Write 65% as a decimal.

*Answer:* _____0.65_____

*Part B*

Write 65% as a fraction in lowest terms.

*Answer:* _____$\frac{13}{20}$_____

Explain how you found your answer.

> To change a percent to a decimal, drop the percent sign and move the decimal two places to the left: 0.65. To change a percent to a fraction, remove the percent sign and put 65 over 100. Then divide the numerator and denominator by 5 to reduce the fraction to $\frac{13}{20}$.

9  Before the Erie Canal was built, it took 20 days to ship goods between New York City and Buffalo. After the canal was completed, this time was reduced by 60%.

*Part A*

Write 60% as a decimal and a fraction in lowest terms.

*Decimal:* _____

*Fraction:* _____

*Part B*

Explain how you found your answers.

_____

_____

_____

**Read the problem. Write your answer for each part.**

**10**  Many battles of the Revolutionary War were fought in New York.
About 20% of all major American victories occurred there.

*Part A*

What does 20% mean?

_____

_____

*Part B*

Write 20% as a decimal.

*Answer:* _____

*Part C*

Write 20% as a fraction in lowest terms.

*Show your work.*

*Answer:* _____

# Ratios

**Indicators** 5.N.6, 7

✓ A **ratio** is a comparison of two numbers.

The ratio of squares to triangles is 3 to 4.

The numbers can be compared several ways.

| | | | |
|---|---|---|---|
| squares to triangles | 3 to 4 | 3:4 | $\frac{3}{4}$ |
| triangles to squares | 4 to 3 | 4:3 | $\frac{4}{3}$ |
| squares to shapes | 3 to 7 | 3:7 | $\frac{3}{7}$ |
| triangles to shapes | 4 to 7 | 4:7 | $\frac{4}{7}$ |

✓ Express a ratio in lowest terms, or simplest form.

To reduce a ratio to lowest terms, find the greatest common factor of the numerator and denominator and divide by that number.

A class has a ratio of boys to girls of $\frac{16}{18}$. What is the ratio in lowest terms?

Factors of 16: 1, **2**, 4, 8, 16
Factors of 18: 1, **2**, 3, 6, 9, 18
Greatest common factor of 16 and 18: 2

$$\frac{16 \div 2}{18 \div 2} = \frac{8}{9}$$

The ratio $\frac{16}{18}$ is equivalent to $\frac{8}{9}$ in lowest terms.

---

*Remember—*

Ratios can be written three ways:

• with the word *to*
  5 to 6

• with a colon
  5:6

• as a fraction
  $\frac{5}{6}$

Read all of these forms as "five to six."

There are three types of ratios:

• whole to part
• part to whole
• part to part

When a fraction is in lowest terms, or simplest form, it cannot be made simpler.

---

**Unit 2** Decimals and Percents

**Read each problem. Circle the letter of the best answer.**

Use the picture below to answer questions 1 and 2.

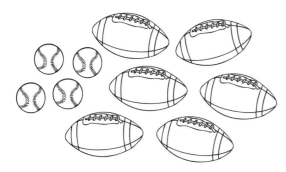

**1**  What is the ratio of baseballs to footballs?

**A**  6 to 4

**B**  4 to 6

**C**  6 to 10

**D**  4 to 10

> The correct answer is B. There are 4 baseballs and 6 footballs, so the ratio of baseballs to footballs is 4 to 6.

**2**  Which of the following ratios is **not** equivalent to the ratio of footballs to all balls?

**A**  3:5

**B**  6 to 10

**C**  2:5

**D**  $\frac{6}{10}$

---

**3**  Hernan had 2 apples, 4 oranges, and 3 bananas. What is the ratio of oranges to the total pieces of fruit he had?

**A**  4:2          **C**  4:3

**B**  4:9          **D**  4:5

**4**  What is the ratio of the letter *a* to the letter *e* in the word *mathematics?*

**A**  $\frac{1}{2}$          **C**  $\frac{11}{2}$

**B**  $\frac{2}{11}$          **D**  $\frac{2}{1}$

**5**  A kennel has 10 puppies for sale. Three of them are poodle puppies. The rest are sheltie puppies. What is the ratio of poodle puppies to all the puppies for sale?

**A**  3:7          **C**  7:3

**B**  3:10          **D**  7:10

**6**  In which set is the ratio of all cards to hearts 3:1?

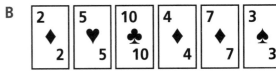

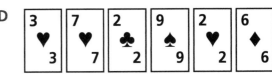

**7**  The Adirondack Park covers about one-fifth of the area of New York State. How is the ratio of the park's area to the state's area expressed?

**A**  5 to 1          **C**  1 to 6

**B**  1 to 4          **D**  1 to 5

**Read each problem. Write your answers.**

**8** Howard has two fish tanks. There are 12 fish in the first tank and 16 fish in the second tank.

*Part A*

What is the ratio of fish in the first tank to the fish in the second tank? Write the ratio three different ways.

*Answer:* ___12 to 16___ and ___12:16___ and ___$\frac{12}{16}$___

*Part B*

What is the ratio of fish in the second tank to the total number of Howard's fish? Write the ratio three different ways.

*Answer:* ___16 to 28___ and ___16:28___ and ___$\frac{16}{28}$___

> Ratios can be expressed using the word *to*, with a colon, and as a fraction. The ratio of fish in the first tank, 12, to fish in the second tank, 16, is 12 to 16, 12:16, and $\frac{12}{16}$. The total number of fish is $12 + 16 = 28$. So the ratio of fish in the second tank, 16, to all fish is 16 to 28, 16:28, and $\frac{16}{28}$.

**9** The cafeteria staff made 500 sandwiches using white bread and 150 sandwiches using whole wheat bread.

*Part A*

What is the ratio of white bread sandwiches to wheat bread sandwiches, expressed in lowest terms?

*Show your work.*

*Answer:* _____

*Part B*

What is the ratio of white bread sandwiches to all sandwiches? Express your answer in lowest terms.

*Answer:* _____

**Unit 2** Decimals and Percents

**Read the problem. Write your answer for each part.**

**10** The table shows the ratio of 5th-grade students to 6th-grade students in four after-school activities.

**AFTER-SCHOOL ACTIVITIES**

| Activity | Ratio Grade 5 to Grade 6 |
|----------|--------------------------|
| Volleyball | 3:4 |
| Band | 12:16 |
| Painting | 6:8 |
| Writing | 2:4 |

*Part A*

What is the ratio of students in the band in lowest terms?

*Show your work.*

> **Ask Yourself**
> What number can I divide the numerator and denominator by to get lowest terms?

*Answer:* _____

*Part B*

Which activity ratio is **not** equivalent to the ratios of the other three activities?

*Answer:* _____

*Part C*

On the lines below, explain why your answer to Part B is correct.

_____

_____

_____

# Decimals and Percents Review

**Read each problem. Circle the letter of the best answer.**

**1** Nearly 80% of all people in upstate New York live within 25 miles of the Erie Canal. How is 80% written as a decimal?

  **A** 8.0       **C** 0.8

  **B** 0.88      **D** 0.08

**2** Jaden weighs one hundred fifteen and four hundredths pounds. Which of these is his weight in standard form?

  **A** 115.40

  **B** 115.44

  **C** 115.404

  **D** 115.04

**3** Which of these is **not** equivalent to 70%?

  **A** 0.07       **C** 0.70

  **B** $\frac{7}{10}$       **D** $\frac{14}{20}$

**4** Which list is ordered from least to greatest?

  **A** 2.037, 2.07, 2.307, 2.7

  **B** 2.7, 2.07, 2.307, 2.037

  **C** 2.307, 2.07, 2.037, 2.7

  **D** 2.07, 2.037, 2.307, 2.7

**5** What is the ratio of the number of sides of a pentagon to the number of sides of a hexagon?

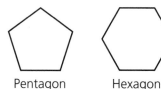

Pentagon        Hexagon

  **A** 1:5       **C** 5:11

  **B** 5:6       **D** 6:5

**6** Which of the following is true?

  **A** 0.345 > 0.435

  **B** 0.761 < 0.716

  **C** 0.112 < 0.012

  **D** 0.869 > 0.857

**7** A group of 12 boys went for ice cream. Four boys got vanilla ice cream and the rest got chocolate. What is the ratio of the boys who got vanilla to all the boys?

  **A** 3:1       **C** 1:2

  **B** 2:1       **D** 1:3

**8** A farm has 200 acres. Of it, 50 acres are planted with soybeans. What percentage of the farm is soybeans?

  **A** 10%       **C** 50%

  **B** 25%       **D** 75%

**Unit 2** Decimals and Percents

**Read each problem. Write your answers.**

**9** The ratio $\frac{3}{5}$ describes students in Ms. Gonzales's class who chose pizza as their favorite food.

**Part A**

What does the ratio $\frac{3}{5}$ mean in this situation?

_____

_____

**Part B**

Express this ratio two other ways.

*Answer:* _____ and _____

**10** Gabby made this table to show the weights of four boxes.

**WEIGHT OF BOXES**

| Box | Weight in Pounds |
|-----|------------------|
| 1 | 4.9 |
| 2 | 4.195 |
| 3 | 4.09 |
| 4 | 4.951 |

**Part A**

List the weights of the boxes in order from least to greatest.

*Answer:* _____

**Part B**

Explain how you know your answer is correct.

_____

_____

_____

**11** Thirty-six percent of all adults in a town voted in the last election.

**Part A**

What does this number mean?

*Answer:* _____

**Part B**

What is this number written as a decimal and as a fraction in lowest terms?

*Decimal:* _____      *Fraction:* _____

**Read the problem. Write your answer for each part.**

**12**  In New York State, there are about twice as many people under 18 years old compared to people over 65 years old.

### Part A

Malcolm said the ratio of people under 18 to people over 65 is about 1 to 2. Is Malcolm correct?

*Answer:* _____

Explain your answer.

_____

_____

### Part B

What is another way to write the ratio?

*Answer:* _____

### Part C

What is the ratio of people over 65 to people under 18?

*Answer:* _____

# Unit 3
## Number Theory

As you work with numbers, you must understand certain characteristics of them. All numbers, except 0 and 1, are either prime or composite. To decide if a number is prime or composite, you must be able to find its factors. Knowing how to find factors and multiples of numbers can help you solve other problems with numbers. To find the value of an expression with more than one operation, you must know the correct order of operations. This unit will help you understand number theory.

Lesson 1  **Primes and Composites** reviews how to decide if a number is prime or composite.

Lesson 2  **Factors and Multiples** reviews how to find multiples and factors of numbers. You will also find the least common multiple and the greatest common factor of pairs of numbers.

Lesson 3  **Order of Operations** reviews the correct order of operations to use when finding the value of an expression.

# Primes and Composites

**Indicator   5.N.12**

✓ A **prime number** has exactly two factors: 1 and itself.

$$2 \quad 5 \quad 7 \quad 13 \quad 29$$

These numbers are primes. The number 2 is the first prime number and the only even prime number. Its factors are 1 and 2.

✓ A **composite number** has three or more factors: 1, itself, and *at least* one other factor. Many composites have more than three factors.

$$4 \quad 8 \quad 20 \quad 64 \quad 125$$

These numbers are composites. For example, the factors of 20 are 1, 2, 4, 5, 10, and 20. The factors of 64 are 1, 2, 4, 8, 16, 32, 64.

✓ A number is **divisible,** or can be divided evenly, by any number that is a factor. A number is divisible by—

- 2 if the ones digit is 0, 2, 4, 6, or 8.

$$\mathbf{14} \quad 560 \quad 3,72\mathbf{8}$$

- 3 if the sum of the digits is divisible by 3.

$$7,521 \rightarrow 7 + 5 + 2 + 1 = 15 \rightarrow 15 \div 3 = 5$$

- 5 if the ones digit is a 5 or 0.

$$215 \quad 11,869,230$$

- 9 if the sum of the digits is divisible by 9.

$$48,924 \rightarrow 4 + 8 + 9 + 2 + 4 = 27 \rightarrow 27 \div 9 = 3$$

- 10 if the ones digit is 0.

$$170 \quad 2,780 \quad 139,250$$

---

*Remember—*

$$\text{Factor} \quad \text{Product}$$
$$\downarrow \qquad \downarrow$$
$$3 \times 4 = 12$$
$$\uparrow$$
$$\text{Factor}$$

**Factors** are the numbers that are multiplied to get a product.

$$1 \times 9 = 9$$
$$3 \times 3 = 9$$

The factors of 9 are 1, 3, and 9.

Except for 2, every even number is composite because it has at least three factors: 1, itself, and 2.

The numbers 0 and 1 are special cases. They do not have two or more factors, so they are neither prime nor composite.

A composite number is divisible by all of its factors.

**Read each problem. Circle the letter of the best answer.**

**1** Which list shows all the prime numbers from 50 to 60?

A   53, 59

B   53, 57, 59

C   51, 53, 55, 57

D   51, 54, 55, 59

The correct answer is A. The numbers 53 and 59 are prime because they have only two factors: 1 and the number itself. All of the other numbers, 51, 52, 54, 55, 56, 57, and 58, are composite because they have at least three factors.

**2** Which of these is a prime number?

A   15

B   16

C   17

D   18

**3** Look at these slips of paper.

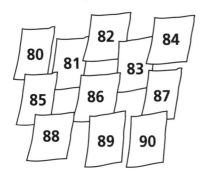

How many slips of paper have prime numbers?

A   one

B   two

C   three

D   four

**4** Which set contains only prime numbers?

A   {12, 31, 42}

B   {13, 14, 19}

C   {11, 37, 41}

D   {21, 25, 33}

**5** The first railroad in the United States ran between Albany and Schenectady. The distance it ran was a prime number less than 15. How many miles could passengers travel on this railroad?

A   6

B   11

C   15

D   23

**6** How many of the numbers on this sign are composite?

**Come to our Class Play!**
June 26
Time: 7 o'clock
Cost: $10

A   none

B   one

C   two

D   three

**7** Which of these is composite?

A   19

B   23

C   47

D   63

**8** Which of these numbers is prime?

A   102

B   123

C   137

D   145

**Read each problem. Write your answers.**

**9** Lorena's parents are between the ages of 40 and 46. Their ages are two prime numbers.

### Part A

What are Lorena's parents' ages?

Answer: _____41_____ and _____43_____

### Part B

Explain how you know your answer is correct.

The numbers between 40 and 46 are 41, 42, 43, 44, and 45. The numbers 42 and 44 are even, so they are composite. Since 45 ends in 5, it is divisible by 5 and is composite. The factors of 41 are 1 and 41 and the factors of 43 are 1 and 43, so they are prime numbers.

**10** There are 58 species of wild orchids growing in New York State.

### Part A

Is 58 a prime number or a composite number?

Answer: _____

Explain your answer.

_____

_____

### Part B

What are the next three prime numbers after 58?

Answer: _____ and _____ and _____

**Unit 3** Number Theory

**Read the problem. Write your answer for each part.**

**11** Mr. Bush sells marbles at toy shows. He has many different kinds
of marbles in several different colors. He has 265 blue marbles,
117 yellow marbles, 132 red marbles, and 241 green marbles.

### Part A

Which color marbles can Mr. Bush display evenly in rows of 5?
Which can he display evenly in rows of 9?

*Rows of 5:* _____

*Rows of 9:* _____

Explain how you know your answers are correct.

_____

_____

_____

### Part B

Which number of marbles is a prime number?

*Answer:* _____

Explain how you know.

_____

_____

> **Ask Yourself**
> What are factors of
> each of the number
> of marbles?

# Factors and Multiples

**Indicators** 5.N.13, 14, 15

**Multiples** are the product of a whole number and another whole number.

$$1 \times 6 = 6 \qquad 2 \times 6 = 12 \qquad 3 \times 6 = 18$$

6, 12, and 18 are multiples of 6.

**Common multiples** are multiples shared by two or more numbers.

Multiples of 3: 3, **6,** 9, **12,** …
Multiples of 6: **6, 12,** 18, 24, …
Common multiples of 3 and 6: 6, 12, …

The **least common multiple** (LCM) of two numbers is the smallest multiple they share.

Multiples of 5: 5, **10,** 15, 20, 25, 30, …
Multiples of 10: **10,** 20, 30, 40, …
Least common multiple of 5 and 10: 10

To find the LCM of two numbers, find multiples of each number and identify the smallest multiple that both numbers have in common.

**Common factors** are factors shared by two or more numbers.

Factors of 28: **1, 2, 4,** 7, 14, 28
Factors of 32: **1, 2, 4,** 8, 16, 32
Common factors of 28 and 32: 1, 2, and 4

The **greatest common factor** (GCF) is the largest factor two numbers share.

The GCF of 28 and 32 is 4.

To find the GCF of two numbers, first find all the factors and identify common factors. Then look for the largest common factors.

---

*Remember—*

A **product** is the answer to a multiplication problem.

$$\overset{\text{Factors}}{\underset{\downarrow\quad\downarrow}{}}$$
$$7 \times 6 = 42$$
$$\underset{\text{Product}}{\uparrow}$$

All even numbers have even multiples.

$$1 \times 4 = 4 \qquad 2 \times 4 = 8$$
$$3 \times 4 = 12 \qquad 4 \times 4 = 16$$

Odd numbers may have both odd and even multiples.

$$1 \times 5 = 5 \qquad 2 \times 5 = 10$$
$$3 \times 5 = 15 \qquad 4 \times 5 = 20$$

**Factors** are numbers that are multiplied together to get a product.

$$1 \times 25 = 25 \qquad 5 \times 5 = 25$$

1, 5, and 25 are factors of 25.

Factors always include 1 and the number itself.

Factors of 4: 1, 2, 4

---

**Unit 3** Number Theory

**Read each problem. Circle the letter of the best answer.**

**1** What is the greatest common factor (GCF) of 36 and 54?

A  2

C  9

B  4

D  18

The correct answer is D. First find all the factors of 36 and 54. Factors of 36: 1, 2, 3, 4, 6, 9, 12, 18, 36. Factors of 54: 1, 2, 3, 6, 9, 18, 27, 54. The greatest common factor of both 36 and 54 is 18.

**2** There are about 722 miles of subway tracks in New York City. Which of these is a factor of 722?

A  2

B  4

C  5

D  6

**3** Maria and Jamal bought some boxes of colored pencils. Each box contains the same number of pencils. If Maria bought 21 pencils and Jamal bought 35, how many pencils were in each box?

A  1

C  5

B  3

D  7

**4** Which number is a common multiple of 9 and 12?

A  18

B  36

C  48

D  54

**5** Oranges come in bags of 10. Apples come in bags of 15. Marty wants to buy an equal number of each type of fruit. What is the smallest number of oranges and apples he can buy?

A  10

B  15

C  20

D  30

**6** Which set shows all the factors of 48?

A  {2, 4, 6, 8, 10, 12, 14, 16}

B  {1, 2, 3, 4, 12, 16, 24, 48}

C  {1, 2, 3, 4, 6, 8, 12, 16, 24, 48}

D  {1, 2, 3, 4, 6, 7, 8, 9, 10, 12, 48}

**7** What is the greatest common factor (GCF) of 42 and 56?

A  2

B  7

C  8

D  14

**8** How many multiples of 8 are less than 50?

A  four

B  five

C  six

D  seven

**Read each problem. Write your answers.**

**9** There are 15 seats in each row of an auditorium.

### Part A

How many total seats are in the first four rows of the auditorium?

*Row 1:* _____15_____    *Row 2:* _____30_____

*Row 3:* _____45_____    *Row 4:* _____60_____

### Part B

Explain how you know your answer is correct.

> Since each row has 15 seats, the answers must be multiples of 15: $1 \times 15 = 15$, $2 \times 15 = 30$, $3 \times 15 = 45$, $4 \times 15 = 60$.

**10** Look at these two numbers.

64     58

### Part A

What is the greatest common factor (GCF) of 64 and 58?

*Show your work.*

*Answer:* _____

### Part B

On the lines below, explain how you found your answer.

_____

_____

_____

**Read the problem. Write your answer for each part.**

**11** A youth soccer league has 400 players. A traveling team is made up of 120 of those players.

### Part A

What are the factors of 400 and 120?

*Factors of 400:* _____

_____

*Factors of 120:* _____

### Part B

What are the common factors of 400 and 120?

*Answer:* _____

### Part C

What is the greatest common factor of 400 and 120?

*Answer:* _____

Explain why your answer is correct.

_____

_____

_____

_____

# Order of Operations

**Indicator   5.N.18   CCSS   5.OA.1**

✓ When an expression has more than one operation, complete the operations in a certain order.

First complete the operations inside **parentheses.**

$$(7 + 3) \div 2 + 6$$
$$10 \div 2 + 6$$

Next, multiply or divide in order from left to right.

$$10 \div 2 + 6$$
$$5 + 6$$

Finally, add or subtract in order from left to right.

$$5 + 6$$
$$11$$

If there are no parentheses, multiply or divide from left to right first. Then add or subtract from left to right.

$$9 - 2 \times 3 + 2$$
$$9 - 6 + 2$$
$$3 + 2$$
$$5$$

✓ **Inverse operations** are opposite operations that undo each other.

Addition and subtraction are inverse operations. You can add to check subtraction or subtract to check addition.

$$64 - 4 = 60$$
because
$$60 + 4 = 64$$

Multiplication and division are also inverse operations. You can multiply to check division and divide to check multiplication.

$$56 \div 7 = 8$$
because
$$8 \times 7 = 56$$

*Remember—*

Parentheses ( ) are grouping symbols. *Always* work inside parentheses first.

The **commutative property** says that numbers may be added or multiplied in any order.

$$23 + 12 = 12 + 23$$
$$4 \times 6 = 6 \times 4$$

The commutative property is *not* true for subtraction or division.

The **associative property** says numbers can be grouped in any order to add or multiply.

$$(4 + 7) + 3 = 4 + (7 + 3)$$
$$2 \times (6 \times 5) = (2 \times 6) \times 5$$

**Unit 3** Number Theory

**Read each problem. Circle the letter of the best answer.**

**1** Janelle used this expression to find the total cost of a $10 book and 4 binders for $5 each.

$$10 + 5 \times 4$$

How much did Janelle spend in all?

**A** $19  **C** $54

**B** $30  **D** $60

The correct answer is B. There are no parentheses, so multiply or divide first: $5 \times 4 = 20$. Then add or subtract: $10 + 20 = 30$. Janelle spent $30 in all.

**2** What is the value of this expression?

$$7 \times 2 + 7$$

**A** 16  **C** 63

**B** 21  **D** 98

**3** What number makes the number sentence true?

$$(6 \times \square) \div 2 + 4 = 13$$

**A** 1  **C** 3

**B** 2  **D** 4

**4** Which of these expressions has the greatest value?

**A** $(8 \times 9) \times (6 \times 2)$

**B** $(8 + 9) \times (6 + 2)$

**C** $8 \times (9 \times 6) + 2$

**D** $8 + (9 \times 6) \times 2$

**5** Which of these expressions will result in the smallest value?

**A** $4 \times 2 - 1$

**B** $4 + 2 - 1$

**C** $4 \div 2 + 1$

**D** $4 \div 2 - 1$

**6** Which of these number sentences is true?

**A** $(4 \times 5) + 3 = 19$

**B** $(6 \div 2) \times 7 = 20$

**C** $(5 \times 7) - 4 = 35$

**D** $(6 \times 8) - 5 = 43$

**7** Which of these expressions results in 315?

**A** $300 \div (2 \times 4) - 285$

**B** $(300 \div 2) \times 4 - 285$

**C** $(300 + 2) \div 4 + 285$

**D** $(300 \times 2) \div 4 + 285$

**8** Look at this expression.

$$18 + (3 \times 3) \div 9$$

What is the correct order of operations to find the value of the expression?

**A** add, multiply, divide

**B** multiply, divide, add

**C** multiply, add, divide

**D** divide, multiply, add

**Read each problem. Write your answers.**

**9** Look at this expression.

$$2 \times (100 + 200)$$

**Part A**

What is the value of the expression?

Answer: _____600_____

**Part B**

What would the value of the expression be if the parentheses were removed?

Answer: _____400_____

> Using the order of operations, do work inside the parentheses first: $100 + 200 = 300$. Then multiply: $2 \times 300 = 600$. If the parentheses were removed, the first operation would be multiplication: $2 \times 100$. Then addition: $200 + 200 = 400$.

**10** Juanita wrote the following expression on the board.

$$60 - (14 \div 2) \times 3$$

What is the value of Juanita's expression?

**Show your work.**

Answer: _____

**Read the problem. Write your answer for each part.**

11  Look at this expression.

$$(3 + 9) \div 3 \times 2 - 3$$

**Part A**

What is the value of the expression?

*Answer:* _____

*Ask Yourself*
What operation do I
perform first?

**Part B**

On the lines below, explain the steps you used to find your answer.

_____

_____

_____

_____

**Part C**

If the parentheses in the expression above were removed, what would
be the value of the expression?

*Answer:* _____

**Read each problem. Circle the letter of the best answer.**

**1** What is the value of this expression?

$$30 \div 6 - 1$$

**A** 3          **C** 5

**B** 4          **D** 6

**2** Shelby is packing softballs in cartons. If she packed 30 softballs in a carton, how many softballs would be packed in the first four cartons?

**A** 30, 40, 50, 60

**B** 30, 50, 70, 90

**C** 30, 60, 90, 120

**D** 30, 90, 120, 150

**3** What is the greatest common factor (GCF) of 16 and 24?

**A** 2          **C** 6

**B** 4          **D** 8

**4** What is the set of all the factors of 124?

**A** {1, 2, 4, 6, 8, 31, 124}

**B** {1, 4, 6, 31, 62, 124}

**C** {2, 4, 8, 16, 62, 124}

**D** {1, 2, 4, 31, 62, 124}

**5** What is the value of $7 + 7 \times 8 - 2$?

**A** 20          **C** 84

**B** 61          **D** 110

**6** How many multiples of 7 are less than 70?

**A** seven

**B** eight

**C** nine

**D** ten

**7** Which of these is a prime number?

**A** 25          **C** 31

**B** 27          **D** 39

**8** Look at this expression.

$$8 \times (9 + 3) \div 2$$

What is the correct order of operations to find the value of the expression?

**A** multiply, add, divide

**B** add, divide, multiply

**C** add, multiply, divide

**D** divide, multiply, add

**9** Which of the following is a composite number?

**A** 121          **C** 409

**B** 211          **D** 503

**Read each problem. Write your answers.**

**10** Look at this expression.

$$8 + 4 \times (7 - 1) \div 2$$

What is the value of the expression?

***Show your work.***

*Answer:* _____

**11** Angelo had bags of apples and oranges. There were a total of 98 apples and 126 oranges.

*Part A*

What are the factors of 98 and 126?

***Factors of 98:*** _____

***Factors of 126:*** _____

*Part B*

What are the common factors of 98 and 126?

*Answer:* _____

**12** The Statue of Liberty is huge, with an index finger that is 8 feet long. Its head is 10 feet wide from ear to ear and the mouth is 3 feet wide!

*Part A*

What are the first ten multiples of 3 and 8?

***Multiples of 3:*** _____

***Multiples of 8:*** _____

*Part B*

What is the least common multiple (LCM) of 3 and 8?

*Answer:* _____

**Read the problem. Write your answer for each part.**

**13** Watkins Glen State Park is centered around a gorge. A stream runs through it, creating 19 waterfalls. Trails along the gorge create walking paths through the falls.

**Part A**

What are the factors of 19?

*Answer:* _____

Is the number 19 prime or composite? Why?

_____

_____

**Part B**

At one place along the trail, a side stream joins the main stream to form Rainbow Falls, which drops 110 feet.

What are the factors of 110?

*Answer:* _____

Is the number 110 prime or composite? Why?

_____

_____

**Part C**

Triple Cascade drops 26 feet. What is the greatest common factor (GCF) of 26 and 110?

*Answer:* _____

# Unit 4
## Operations

Addition, subtraction, multiplication, and division are operations. You can do these operations with whole numbers, decimals, and fractions. When you work with different types of numbers, you follow different steps. It is important to be able to perform these operations correctly with all types of numbers. This unit will help you add, subtract, multiply, and divide numbers.

**Lesson 1** **Multiplying Three-Digit Numbers** reviews how to multiply a three-digit whole number by another three-digit whole number.

**Lesson 2** **Dividing Three-Digit Numbers** reviews how to divide a three-digit whole number by a one- or two-digit whole number.

**Lesson 3** **Renaming Fractions and Mixed Numbers** reviews how to put fractions into lowest terms. You will also change a mixed number to an improper fraction and an improper fraction to a mixed number.

**Lesson 4** **Adding and Subtracting Fractions and Mixed Numbers** reviews adding and subtracting fractions and mixed numbers with like denominators.

**Lesson 5** **Operations with Decimals** reviews how to add, subtract, multiply, and divide decimals.

# Multiplying Three-Digit Numbers

**Indicator** 5.N.16 **CCSS** 5.NBT.5

✓ Multiply whole numbers from right to left.

To multiply a three-digit number, first multiply by the ones to find a partial product. Then multiply by the tens to find a second partial product. Finally, multiply by hundreds to find a third partial product. Add the partial products to find the total.

A certain model of washer sells for $632. A store sold 215 of these washers in one year. What were the total sales on this model of washer?

$632
×215
3160

Multiply by the ones: 5 × 632 = 10 + 150 + 3,000 = 3,160.

$632
×215
3160
6320

Multiply by the tens: 10 × 632 = 20 + 300 + 6,000 = 6,320.

$632
×215
3160
6320
126400

Multiply by the hundreds: 200 × 632 = 400 + 6,000 + 120,000 = 126,400.

$632
×215
3160
6320
126400
$135,880

Add the partial products: 3,160 + 6,320 + 126,400 = 135,880

The total sales of the washer were $135,880.

**Remember—**

Crutch numbers can help you remember regrouped values. When you regroup in multiplication, add the crutch number *after* you multiply the digit in that place.

4 1
273
×6
1,638

153
×724
612 ← Partial product
3060 ← Partial product
107100 ← Partial product
110,772 ← Product

**Read each problem. Circle the letter of the best answer.**

**1** What is the product of 236 × 432?

   **A** 10,952

   **B** 19,952

   **C** 101,952

   **D** 191,952

> The correct answer is C. Multiply by the ones: 6 × 432 = 2,592. Next, multiply by the tens: 30 × 432 = 12,960. Last, multiply by the hundreds: 200 × 432 = 86,400. Add the partial products: 2,592 + 12,960 + 86,400 = 101,952.

**2** A truck driver drove 932 miles on a delivery route one week. If he drove this route for 6 weeks, how many miles did he drive?

   **A** 5,482

   **B** 5,592

   **C** 6,642

   **D** 54,192

**3** A bakery produces 810 loaves of bread a day. How many loaves will it produce in 23 days?

   **A** 1,620

   **B** 4,050

   **C** 18,630

   **D** 19,730

**4** An average of 157 customers enter a certain shoe store each day. How many customers will enter the store during 124 days?

   **A** 19,368

   **B** 19,468

   **C** 19,528

   **D** 19,668

**5** Which is *not* a step in finding the product of 239 × 327?

   **A** 9 × 327

   **B** 30 × 327

   **C** 200 × 327

   **D** 3 × 239

**6** A hotel room rents for $250 a night. It is booked every day for 131 days. How much money will be taken in on the room for those days?

   **A** $3,275

   **B** $32,750

   **C** $37,500

   **D** $375,000

**7** Maddy is multiplying 215 × 536. Which step did she do incorrectly?

   **A** 5 × 536 = 2,680

   **B** 10 × 536 = 53,600

   **C** 200 × 536 = 107,200

   **D** 2,680 + 5,360 = 8,040

**Read each problem. Write your answers.**

**8** Brenda is a travel agent. She signed up 167 people for a bus tour that costs $455 per person.

What is the cost of the bus tour for all the people?

*Show your work.*

$$
\begin{array}{r}
455 \\
\times 167 \\
\hline
3185 \\
27300 \\
45500 \\
\hline
75{,}985
\end{array}
$$

*Answer:* $ _____75,985_____

> To find the total cost, multiply the number of people on the tour and the cost of the tour per person. First multiply the ones for a partial product: $7 \times 455 = 3{,}185$. Multiply the tens: $60 \times 455 = 27{,}300$. Then multiply the hundreds: $100 \times 455 = 45{,}500$. Finally, add the partial products: $3{,}185 + 27{,}300 + 45{,}500 = 75{,}985$. The total cost is $75,985.

**9** One city has 30 museums and galleries to visit.

*Part A*

If each of the museums and galleries attracts an average of 763 visitors a week, how many people visit the museums and galleries in one week?

*Answer:* _____ people

*Part B*

If each of the museums and galleries attracted an average of 29 more visitors, how many **more** people would visit in a week?

*Show your work.*

*Answer:* _____ people

Unit 4 Operations

**Read the problem. Write your answer for each part.**

**10** Rocco's parents bought a new house. They will make monthly payments of $725 for 360 months.

### Part A

How much will Rocco's parents have paid after 360 months?

*Show your work.*

> **Ask Yourself**
> How many hundreds, tens, and ones are in the number 360?

*Answer:* $_____

### Part B

Explain why your answer is correct.

_____

_____

_____

### Part C

Rocco's parents had been making payments of $856 for 240 months on their old house. Which house would cost Rocco's parents more money? Explain your answer.

_____

_____

_____

_____

# Dividing Three-Digit Numbers

**Indicator   5.N.17   CCSS   5.NBT.6**

✓ Divide whole numbers from left to right. To divide by a two-digit number, first round the divisor to the nearest ten and estimate the quotient. Then multiply, subtract, and repeat.

A small bakery made 448 pies in 28 days. What was the average number of pies it made per day?

$$
\begin{array}{r}
16 \\
28\overline{)448} \\
28 \\
\hline
168 \\
168 \\
\hline
\end{array}
$$

Think of 450 ÷ 30 = 15. The quotient starts in the tens place. Try 1. Multiply: 1 × 28 = 28.
Subtract: 44 − 28 = 16. Bring down the 8.
Estimate: 180 ÷ 30 = 6. Try 6.
Multiply: 6 × 28 = 168.
Subtract: 168 − 168 = 0.

The bakery made an average of 16 pies a day.

✓ Sometimes a number does not divide evenly and there is a **remainder** in the quotient. Interpret remainders in word problems carefully. Sometimes you can drop the remainder.

The bakery made 340 cupcakes and packed them in boxes of 24. How many boxes were filled?

$$
\begin{array}{r}
14\,R4 \\
24\overline{)340} \\
24 \\
\hline
100 \\
96 \\
\hline
4
\end{array}
$$

A total of 14 boxes were filled and 4 cupcakes were left over.

Other times you will need to round the quotient up.

Greta needs 340 cookies. The cookies come in bags of 24. How many bags should Greta buy?

$$
\begin{array}{r}
14\,R4 \\
24\overline{)340} \\
24 \\
\hline
100 \\
96 \\
\hline
4
\end{array}
$$

Greta needs 4 more cookies than are in 14 bags, so round up to 15 bags.

## Remember—

The **dividend** is the number being divided. The **divisor** is the number doing the dividing. The **quotient** is the result.

$$
\begin{array}{cc}
\text{Dividend} & \text{Quotient} \\
\downarrow & \downarrow \\
128 \div 8 & = 16 \\
& \uparrow \\
& \text{Divisor}
\end{array}
$$

$$
\begin{array}{r}
16 \leftarrow \text{Quotient} \\
8\overline{)128} \\
\uparrow \ \ \uparrow
\end{array}
$$

Divisor   Dividend

Make sure to begin the quotient in the correct place. Put it above the place you are dividing.

$$
\begin{array}{r}
20 \\
4\overline{)80}
\end{array}
$$

8 tens divided by 4 is 2 tens, so write 2 above the tens.

$$
\begin{array}{r}
8 \\
6\overline{)48}
\end{array}
$$

4 tens cannot be divided by 6, so divide 48 ones by 6. Write the quotient, 8, above the ones place.

Check division by multiplying.

$$
180 \div 10 = 18
$$
because
$$
18 \times 10 = 180
$$

**Unit 4** Operations

**Read each problem. Circle the letter of the best answer.**

**1** In a recycling drive, Usie collected 630 aluminum cans. If he got a discount food coupon for every 35 cans he collected, how many coupons did Usie receive?

   **A** 18

   **B** 19

   **C** 20

   **D** 108

> The correct answer is A. Think of $600 \div 40 = 15$. The quotient starts in the tens place. Try 1. Multiply $1 \times 35 = 35$. Subtract: $63 - 35 = 28$. Bring down the 0. Estimate: $300 \div 40 = 7.5$. Try 8. Multiply: $8 \times 35 = 280$. Subtract: $280 - 280 = 0$. Usie received 18 coupons.

**2** What is the smallest three-digit number that can be divided by 7 and have no remainder?

   **A** 101

   **B** 103

   **C** 105

   **D** 112

**3** Ms. Chang needs to pack 378 books into crates for the library book sale. If she can fit 24 books in a crate, how many crates will Ms. Chang need?

   **A** 13

   **B** 14

   **C** 15

   **D** 16

**4** Bulletin board supplies for 6 classrooms cost a total of $846. What was the cost of bulletin board supplies per classroom?

   **A** $121

   **B** $131

   **C** $141

   **D** $151

**5** The Guaranty Building in Buffalo used to be the tallest building in the city, rising to a height of 152 feet. If the Guaranty Building has 13 stories, about how many feet tall is each story?

   **A** 10

   **B** 12

   **C** 14

   **D** 16

**6** Mrs. Vance needs 356 square tiles to cover the kitchen floor. The tiles come in boxes of 12. How many boxes does Mrs. Vance need?

   **A** 27

   **B** 28

   **C** 29

   **D** 30

**7** At Phillips Elementary School, there are 130 fifth-grade students. If there are 5 classes, what is the average number of students in each fifth-grade class?

   **A** 23       **C** 25

   **B** 24       **D** 26

**Read each problem. Write your answers.**

8   The Tindall family drove 436 miles in 7 hours.

   *Part A*

   What is their average speed per hour?

   *Answer:* _____62_____ miles per hour

   *Part B*

   Explain how you found your answer.

   Set up a division problem: 7)436. Decide which place the first digit of the quotient will go in. You can't divide 4 hundreds by 7, so look to the next place, the tens. You can divide 43 tens by 7, so the quotient starts in the tens place. Try 6. Multiply: $7 \times 6 = 42$. Subtract: $43 - 42 = 1$. Bring down the ones, 6, and repeat. Multiply: $2 \times 7 = 14$. Subtract: $16 - 14 = 2$. The remainder is 2. Round down the quotient, 62. The speed is 62 miles per hour.

$$\begin{array}{r} 62 \\ 7\overline{)436} \\ \underline{42} \\ 16 \\ \underline{14} \\ 2 \end{array}$$

9   There were a total of 529 people in the gym for a pep rally. A row of bleachers seats 15 people.

   *Part A*

   How many rows of bleachers were needed to seat all the people?

   **Show your work.**

   *Answer:* _____ rows of bleachers

   *Part B*

   Explain why your answer is correct.

   _____

   _____

**Read the problem. Write your answer for each part.**

10  A short section of the Appalachian Trail passes through New York
State. One summer day, 764 people were counted hiking on this
section of the trail.

### Part A

If these people were counted during an 8-hour period, what was the
average number of hikers each hour?

*Show your work.*

**Ask Yourself**
What is the
divisor? What is the
dividend?

*Answer:* _____ hikers

### Part B

Explain how you found your answer.

_____

_____

_____

### Part C

What is the remainder?

*Answer:* _____

# Renaming Fractions and Mixed Numbers

**Indicators  5.N.19, 20**

✓ When a fraction is in lowest terms, it cannot be made simpler.

To find an equivalent fraction in lowest terms, divide the numerator and denominator by the greatest common factor (GCF).

$$\frac{20}{24} \rightarrow \frac{20 \div 4}{24 \div 4} = \frac{5}{6}$$

Factors of 20: 1, 2, **4,** 5, 10, 20
Factors of 24: 1, 2, 3, **4,** 6, 8, 12, 24
Greatest common factor of 20 and 24: 4

The fraction $\frac{20}{24}$ is equivalent to $\frac{5}{6}$ in lowest terms.

✓ An **improper fraction** has a numerator that is equal to or greater than the denominator. It represents a number that is equal to or greater than 1.

A pizzeria cuts its pizzas into 6 slices each. One hour, the pizzeria sold 9 slices. What fraction names this number?

$$\frac{9}{6} \begin{array}{l} \leftarrow \text{Slices of pizza sold} \\ \leftarrow \text{Slices in a whole} \end{array}$$

An improper fraction can be rewritten as a **mixed number,** that is, a whole number plus a fraction.

First divide the numerator by the denominator to find the whole number. Then write the remainder over the denominator for the fraction.

$$\frac{9}{6} \rightarrow \begin{array}{r} 1 \text{ R3} = 1\frac{3}{6} \text{ or } 1\frac{1}{2} \\ 6\overline{)9} \\ \underline{6} \\ 3 \end{array}$$

$\frac{9}{6}$ is the same as $1\frac{1}{2}$ pizzas.

## Remember—

**Equivalent fractions** name the same number in different terms.

The greatest common factor (GCF) is the largest factor shared by two numbers.

To find the GCF, first find all the factors and identify the common factors. Then look for the largest common factor.

$$\frac{4}{10} = \frac{2}{5}$$

Factors of 4: 1, 2, 4
Factors of 10: 1, 2, 5, 10
GCF of 4 and 10: 2

$$\frac{4}{10} \div \frac{2}{2} = \frac{2}{5}$$

A fraction with a numerator equal to or greater than the denominator is sometimes called an improper fraction.

$$\frac{7}{4} = 1\frac{3}{4}$$

$$\frac{18}{12} = 1\frac{6}{12} = 1\frac{1}{2}$$

To change a mixed number to an improper fraction, multiply the denominator by the whole number and add the numerator. The denominator stays the same.

$$^{+}_{\times}\overset{\frown}{3\frac{5}{6}} = \frac{23}{6}$$

**Read each problem. Circle the letter of the best answer.**

**1** Which of these fractions is in lowest terms?

  **A** $\frac{5}{9}$        **C** $\frac{6}{12}$

  **B** $\frac{4}{10}$       **D** $\frac{9}{15}$

The correct answer is A. The greatest common factor of 5 and 9 is 1. The fraction $\frac{5}{9}$ cannot be made simpler. The GCF of 4 and 10 is 2, so $\frac{4}{10}$ reduces to $\frac{2}{5}$. The GCF of 6 and 12 is 6, so $\frac{6}{12}$ reduces to $\frac{1}{2}$. The GCF of 9 and 15 is 3, so $\frac{9}{15}$ reduces to $\frac{3}{5}$.

**2** Liz lives $1\frac{1}{5}$ miles from the mall. Which improper fraction is equivalent to $1\frac{1}{5}$?

  **A** $\frac{4}{3}$        **C** $\frac{6}{5}$

  **B** $\frac{5}{4}$        **D** $\frac{7}{6}$

**3** A dog had a litter of 12 puppies. Three of the puppies were female and the rest were male. What fraction names the part of the litter that were male puppies in lowest terms?

  **A** $\frac{1}{2}$        **C** $\frac{2}{3}$

  **B** $\frac{1}{3}$        **D** $\frac{3}{4}$

**4** What is the fraction $\frac{24}{36}$ in lowest terms?

  **A** $\frac{12}{18}$       **C** $\frac{2}{3}$

  **B** $\frac{6}{9}$        **D** $\frac{1}{2}$

**5** Alexandra used $4\frac{3}{4}$ feet of wood to make a picture frame. How is $4\frac{3}{4}$ written as an improper fraction?

  **A** $\frac{10}{4}$       **C** $\frac{16}{4}$

  **B** $\frac{13}{4}$       **D** $\frac{19}{4}$

**6** Which choice is true?

  **A** $1\frac{1}{8} = \frac{10}{8}$       **C** $3\frac{2}{3} = \frac{12}{3}$

  **B** $2\frac{4}{5} = \frac{14}{5}$       **D** $4\frac{8}{9} = \frac{42}{9}$

**7** What is the first step in converting an improper fraction to a mixed number?

  **A** Divide the denominator by the numerator.

  **B** Place the remainder over the original denominator.

  **C** Divide the numerator by the denominator.

  **D** Find the greatest common factor of both numbers.

**8** A diner cuts its pies into 8 slices each. One day at lunch, the diner sold 14 slices of pie. What is this fraction of slices sold as a mixed number in lowest terms?

  **A** $1\frac{3}{4}$       **C** $2\frac{1}{3}$

  **B** $1\frac{2}{3}$       **D** $2\frac{1}{4}$

**Read each problem. Write your answers.**

**9** The record for the boys' county indoor high jump is $7\frac{1}{3}$ feet.

**Part A**

Write this height as an improper fraction.

**Show your work.**

$$7\frac{1}{3}$$
$$3 \times 7 = 21$$
$$21 + 1 = 22$$
$$\frac{22}{3}$$

Answer: _____ $\frac{22}{3}$ _____

**Part B**

Explain your answer.

To change the mixed number $7\frac{1}{3}$ to an improper fraction, multiply 7 by 3, which equals 21. Next, add $21 + 1 = 22$, which is the numerator over a denominator of 3. So, $7\frac{1}{3} = \frac{22}{3}$.

**10** A youth group ate 32 of 40 slices of pizza at a weekend retreat.

**Part A**

What fraction of the slices did the group eat? Express your answer in lowest terms.

**Show your work.**

Answer: _____

**Part B**

What is another fraction that has the same lowest terms as $\frac{32}{40}$?

Answer: _____

**Read the problem. Write your answer for each part.**

**11** Mrs. Springborn wanted to make a cheesecake. The recipe called for $2\frac{1}{2}$ pounds of softened cream cheese.

### Part A

What is this amount of cream cheese written as an improper fraction?

*Show your work.*

*Ask Yourself*
What operations do I use to change a mixed number to an improper fraction?

*Answer:* _____

### Part B

Later, Mrs. Springborn decided to triple the recipe to make 3 cheesecakes. The amount of cream cheese needed for 3 cheesecakes is written as an improper fraction of $\frac{15}{2}$. How is this written as a mixed number?

*Show your work.*

*Answer:* _____

✓ To add fractions with like denominators, just add the numerators. The denominator stays the same.

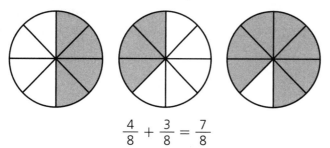

$$\frac{4}{8} + \frac{3}{8} = \frac{7}{8}$$

✓ To subtract fractions with like denominators, subtract the numerators. The denominator stays the same.

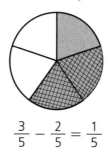

$$\frac{3}{5} - \frac{2}{5} = \frac{1}{5}$$

✓ To add or subtract mixed numbers, first add or subtract the fractions. Then add or subtract the whole numbers.

$$4\frac{5}{7}$$
$$+2\frac{1}{7}$$

$$4\frac{5}{7}$$
$$+2\frac{1}{7}$$
$$\overline{\quad\frac{6}{7}}$$

$$4\frac{5}{7}$$
$$+2\frac{1}{7}$$
$$\overline{6\frac{6}{7}}$$

## Remember—

In a fraction, the top number is the numerator and the bottom number is the denominator.

$$\frac{5}{6} \leftarrow \text{Numerator}$$
$$\phantom{\frac{5}{6}} \leftarrow \text{Denominator}$$

When the numerator and denominator of a fraction are the same, the fraction is equivalent to 1.

$$\frac{6}{6} = 1$$

**Improper fractions** are equal to or greater than 1.

$$\frac{9}{6}$$

**Mixed numbers** include a whole number and a fraction.

$$2\frac{1}{3} \qquad 1\frac{9}{10}$$

To reduce a fraction to lowest terms, or simplest form, find the greatest common factor of the numerator and denominator and divide by that number.

$$\frac{4}{10} = \frac{2}{5}$$

The greatest common factor of 4 and 10 is 2.

$$\frac{4 \div 2}{10 \div 2} = \frac{2}{5}$$

**Unit 4** Operations

**Read each problem. Circle the letter of the best answer.**

1 Last month, Sherri grew $\frac{7}{8}$ inch, while Murali grew $\frac{3}{8}$ inch. How much **more** did Sherri grow than Murali?

A $\frac{1}{4}$ inch    C $\frac{1}{2}$ inch

B $\frac{1}{3}$ inch    D $\frac{2}{3}$ inch

The correct answer is C. To find a difference, subtract: $\frac{7}{8} - \frac{3}{8} = \frac{4}{8}$. Then reduce this fraction to $\frac{1}{2}$.

2 Five-eighths of the lunches sold in a cafeteria were hamburgers. Two-eighths of the lunches were chicken sandwiches. What fraction of the lunches were either hamburgers or chicken sandwiches?

A $\frac{1}{8}$    C $\frac{5}{8}$

B $\frac{3}{8}$    D $\frac{7}{8}$

3 Nine-tenths of Ms. Apple's class chose green as their favorite color. Seven-tenths of Mr. Farber's class also chose green. How much **more** of Ms. Apple's class likes green than Mr. Farber's class?

A $\frac{1}{2}$    C $\frac{1}{6}$

B $\frac{1}{5}$    D $\frac{1}{8}$

4 Which expression has a difference of $\frac{4}{9}$?

A $\frac{8}{9} - \frac{4}{9}$    C $\frac{6}{9} - \frac{3}{9}$

B $\frac{7}{9} - \frac{5}{9}$    D $\frac{5}{9} - \frac{4}{9}$

5 Lake Otisco, in the Finger Lakes region of New York State, is $5\frac{2}{5}$ miles long. Another nearby lake is $6\frac{4}{5}$ miles long. How much shorter is Lake Otisco than the other lake?

A $1\frac{1}{5}$ miles    C $7\frac{3}{5}$ miles

B $1\frac{2}{5}$ miles    D $11\frac{2}{5}$ miles

6 Kendra jogged $2\frac{1}{8}$ miles and Javon jogged $3\frac{3}{8}$ miles. How many miles did they jog in all?

A $5\frac{1}{8}$    C $5\frac{3}{8}$

B $5\frac{2}{8}$    D $5\frac{4}{8}$

7 Which of these number sentences is true?

A $6\frac{1}{3} + 6\frac{1}{3} = 7\frac{2}{3}$

B $8\frac{1}{4} + 8\frac{1}{4} = 12\frac{2}{4}$

C $5\frac{1}{6} + 5\frac{4}{6} = 10\frac{5}{6}$

D $7\frac{3}{8} + 7\frac{3}{8} = 14\frac{6}{16}$

8 Mrs. Cruz bought $\frac{3}{4}$ pound of Swiss cheese and $\frac{3}{4}$ pound of American cheese. How much cheese did she buy in all?

A $\frac{3}{4}$ pound    C $1\frac{1}{2}$ pounds

B $1\frac{1}{4}$ pounds    D 2 pounds

**Read each problem. Write your answers.**

**9** Omar spent $6\frac{3}{4}$ hours mowing the lawn and painting a fence.

If Omar spent $2\frac{1}{4}$ hours mowing the lawn, how many hours did he spend painting? Express your answer in lowest terms.

*Show your work.*

$$6\frac{3}{4}$$
$$-2\frac{1}{4}$$
$$\overline{\phantom{-}4\frac{2}{4}} = 4\frac{1}{2}$$

*Answer:* _____$4\frac{1}{2}$_____ hours

> First set up a subtraction problem. Then subtract the numerators of the fractions, while leaving the denominators the same: $\frac{3}{4} - \frac{1}{4} = \frac{2}{4}$. Next, subtract the whole numbers: $6 - 2 = 4$. The answer is $4\frac{2}{4}$, which you can reduce to simplest form, $4\frac{1}{2}$.

**10** A farmer had a farm of $35\frac{6}{10}$ acres. He purchased a neighboring farm of $29\frac{4}{10}$ acres.

*Part A*

How many acres does the farmer own now?

*Show your work.*

*Answer:* _____ acres

*Part B*

Explain how you found your answer.

_____

_____

_____

**Read the problem. Write your answer for each part.**

11  This table shows the area in square miles of the five boroughs of New York City.

| Borough | Area |
|---------|------|
| Bronx | 44 |
| Brooklyn | $70\frac{6}{10}$ |
| Manhattan | 23 |
| Staten Island | $60\frac{2}{10}$ |
| Queens | $109\frac{2}{10}$ |

*Part A*

What is the combined area of the Bronx and Staten Island?

*Show your work.*

> **Ask Yourself**
> Do I add or subtract to find combined area?

*Answer:* _____ square miles

*Part B*

How much larger is Brooklyn than Staten Island?

*Show your work.*

*Answer:* _____ square miles

*Part C*

How much larger is Queens than the combined areas of the Bronx and Staten Island from Part A?

*Show your work.*

*Answer:* _____ square miles

# Operations with Decimals

**Indicator** 5.N.23 **CCSS** 5.NBT.7

✓ Add or subtract decimals the same way you add or subtract whole numbers, from right to left. Line up the decimal points first, adding placeholder zeros if necessary. Then add or subtract the same places: tenths to tenths, hundredths to hundredths, and so on.

$$4.93 + 5.675 = \square \qquad 17.145 - 8.7 = \square$$

$$
\begin{array}{r}
4.93\mathbf{0} \\
+5.675 \\
\hline
10.605
\end{array}
\qquad
\begin{array}{r}
17.145 \\
-8.7\mathbf{00} \\
\hline
8.445
\end{array}
$$

✓ Multiply decimals the same way you multiply whole numbers. The product will have the same number of decimal places as the sum of the number of places in the factors.

$$6.42 \times 7.29 = \square$$

$$
\begin{array}{r}
7.29 \\
\times 6.42 \\
\hline
1458 \\
2\,9160 \\
+43\,7400 \\
\hline
46.8018
\end{array}
$$

✓ Divide decimals the same way you divide whole numbers. Place the decimal point in the quotient above the decimal point in the dividend.

$$34.95 \div 5 = \square$$

$$
\begin{array}{r}
6.99 \\
5{\overline{)34.95}} \\
\underline{30}\phantom{.95} \\
4\,9\phantom{5} \\
\underline{4\,5}\phantom{5} \\
45 \\
\underline{45}
\end{array}
$$

## Remember—

Use **estimation** to determine if an answer seems reasonable.

Multiplication and division are inverse operations.

$$5{\overline{)3.54}}$$

Think: 5 times what number is 3.54?

Quotient
↓
$$\begin{array}{r} 0.6 \\ 8{\overline{)4.8}} \end{array}$$
↑ ↑
Divisor Dividend

Dividend Quotient
↓ ↓
$$4.8 \div 8 = 0.6$$
↑
Divisor

Dollars and cents are a form of decimal numbers.

Ones  Hundredths
↓   ↓
$$\$4.56$$
↑
Tenths

You can write a whole number in decimal form by adding a decimal point and as many zeros as needed.

$$3 = 3.0 = 3.00 = 3.000$$

**Read each problem. Circle the letter of the best answer.**

**1** What is the sum of 4.98 + 3.7 + 6.381?

   **A** 0.15061     **C** 15.061

   **B** 1.5061     **D** 150.61

The correct answer is C. The addends have different numbers of places, so add placeholder zeros to make them easier to add. Line them up and add from the right.

$$\begin{array}{r} {}^{2\ 1} \\ 4.980 \\ 3.700 \\ +6.381 \\ \hline 15.061 \end{array}$$

The sum is 15.061.

**2** Tomatoes are being sold for $1.89 per pound. How much would 5 pounds of tomatoes cost?

   **A** $5.05     **C** $19.55

   **B** $9.45     **D** $54.45

**3** Tim had a box containing 0.453 kilogram (kg) of salt. He used 0.26 kilogram of the salt for a science experiment. How much salt was left in the box?

   **A** 0.183 kg     **C** 0.427 kg

   **B** 0.193 kg     **D** 0.437 kg

**4** A group of 9 rocks weighs a total of 35.91 pounds. What is the average weight of each rock?

   **A** 0.399 pound

   **B** 3.99 pounds

   **C** 39.9 pounds

   **D** 399 pounds

**5** Ms. James bought 3 world maps for her classroom. The maps cost $24.59 each. What was the total cost of the 3 maps (before tax)?

   **A** $72.77

   **B** $73.57

   **C** $73.77

   **D** $83.57

**6** The athletes competing in a triathlon race will bicycle 15.9 miles, swim 0.75 mile, and run 6.57 miles. What will be the total length of the race?

   **A** 21.12 miles

   **B** 21.22 miles

   **C** 23.12 miles

   **D** 23.22 miles

**7** Janis collected donations for a charity from 26 people in her neighborhood. She collected $202.61. About how much did each person contribute?

   **A** $5     **C** $7

   **B** $6     **D** $8

**8** Find the product.

$$0.8 \times 63.2 = \square$$

   **A** 5.056

   **B** 50.56

   **C** 64.0

   **D** 505.6

**Read each problem. Write your answers.**

**9** Sophora has a total of 30 feet of lumber for a project. If Sophora uses 6.7 feet for the first part of the project and 8.95 feet for the second part, how much lumber is left?

*Show your work.*

$$
\begin{array}{r}
8.95 \\
+6.70 \\
\hline
15.65
\end{array}
\qquad
\begin{array}{r}
30.00 \\
-15.65 \\
\hline
14.35
\end{array}
$$

*Answer:* _____14.35_____ feet

> First add 6.7 and 8.95 to find how many feet of lumber Sophora used for both parts of her project. Then subtract this sum from 30 to find how many feet of lumber are left.

**10** The set director for a community play bought 66 yards of fabric and spent $379.50 (before tax). How much was the cost per yard?

*Show your work.*

*Answer:* $_____

**Read the problem. Write your answer for each part.**

**11**  One rainy day, a stadium sold 1.532 tons of popcorn. The next sunny day, a total of 1.993 tons of popcorn was sold.

### Part A

How much more popcorn was sold on the sunny day?

*Show your work.*

*Ask Yourself*
What operation do I use to find how much more?

*Answer:* _____ ton(s)

### Part B

An average of 1.879 tons of popcorn was sold at each game at the stadium. How many tons of popcorn have been sold at 12 games?

*Answer:* _____ tons

### Part C

Explain how you found your answer to Part B.

_____

_____

_____

_____

# Operations Review

**Read each problem. Circle the letter of the best answer.**

**1** A hotel has 247 rooms. If each room rents for $109 per night, what was the total amount taken in for one night?

A $26,523

C $26,923

B $26,863

D $27,103

**2** One weekend, 32 people walked a total of 384 miles to raise money for a charity. How far did each person walk?

A 11 miles

C 13 miles

B 12 miles

D 14 miles

**3** Tom has 20 cookies. There are 5 chocolate chip, 3 oatmeal-raisin, 4 sugar cookies, and some peanut butter cookies. What fraction of the cookies are peanut butter?

A $\frac{1}{5}$

C $\frac{3}{5}$

B $\frac{2}{5}$

D $\frac{4}{5}$

**4** Jasmine sold $\frac{5}{8}$ of her tickets to the concert. Joanna sold $\frac{7}{8}$ of her tickets. What is the difference in how many of her tickets each girl sold?

A $\frac{1}{8}$

C $\frac{1}{3}$

B $\frac{1}{4}$

D $\frac{1}{2}$

**5** Which is equivalent to $\frac{19}{4}$?

A $3\frac{1}{4}$

C $4\frac{2}{4}$

B $4\frac{1}{4}$

D $4\frac{3}{4}$

**6** The table below shows the amount of fruit Vince bought the other day.

| Fruit | Pounds |
|---|---|
| Grapes | $2\frac{1}{8}$ |
| Bananas | $3\frac{3}{8}$ |
| Peaches | $2\frac{1}{8}$ |

What is the total weight of the fruit Vince bought?

A $5\frac{7}{8}$ pounds

C $7\frac{5}{8}$ pounds

B $6\frac{3}{8}$ pounds

D $9\frac{5}{8}$ pounds

**7** Rummel packed 4 suitcases for a trip. Their total weight was 98.4 pounds. What was the average weight of a suitcase?

A 24.6 pounds

C 24.8 pounds

B 24.7 pounds

D 24.9 pounds

**8** Nick bought 6 packages of gum for $0.85 each. There was no tax. What was the total cost of the 6 packages of gum?

A $4.80

C $5.10

B $4.85

D $5.15

**Read each problem. Write your answers.**

**9** Celine lives $3\frac{2}{10}$ miles from Jeremy and $1\frac{2}{10}$ miles from Terrell.

How much farther does Celine live from Jeremy than from Terrell?

*Show your work.*

*Answer:* _____ miles

**10** From 1929 to 1939, 255 playgrounds were built in New York City.

*Part A*

If an average of 25 workers helped build each playground, how many workers built playgrounds?

*Answer:* _____ workers

*Part B*

Explain how you found your answer.

_____

_____

_____

**11** Mark spent $3\frac{3}{5}$ hours doing chores around the house. He also spent $1\frac{1}{5}$ hours shopping.

How much **more** time did he spend doing chores than shopping? Express your answer in lowest terms.

*Show your work.*

*Answer:* _____ hours

**Unit 4** Operations

83

**Read the problem. Write your answer for each part.**

**12** The New York Stock Exchange has a rating system called an index, which is used to keep track of how well the stocks are doing. One day in July, the New York Stock Exchange Index had a high value of 7,442.32 and a low value of 7,393.3.

*Part A*

What was the difference between the high and low values?

*Show your work.*

*Answer:* _____

*Part B*

The stock exchange is open for 6 hours each day, from Monday to Friday. What was the average change in the index each hour on the day in July?

*Answer:* _____

*Part C*

Explain how you found your answer to Part B.

_____

_____

_____

_____

# Unit 5
## Estimation

Sometimes you do not need to find an exact answer. Then you can use estimation to find an approximate answer. To make a good estimate, you must be able to accurately round numbers. You might estimate the difference between your height and your older brother's height. You might round the number of miles from your house to your grandparents' house. When you read an estimate, you must be able to decide if it is reasonable or not. This unit will help you understand estimation.

Lesson 1 **Rounding and Whole Number Estimation** reviews how to round whole numbers and decimals to a particular place. You will also estimate using whole numbers and decide if estimates are reasonable.

Lesson 2 **Estimating with Fractions** reviews how to round fractions. You will add and subtract with rounded fractions and decide if the estimate is reasonable.

Lesson 3 **Estimating with Decimals** reviews how to estimate sums, differences, products, and quotients of decimals. You will also decide if estimates are reasonable.

# Rounding and Whole Number Estimation

**Indicators** 5.N.24, 27   **CCSS** 5.NBT.4

✓ To **round** a number to a particular place, look at the digit in the **next** place to the right. If it is 4 or lower, round down. If it is 5 or higher, round up.

What is 5,793 rounded to the nearest thousand?

Look at the digit in the hundreds place: 5,**7**93.

The digit is 7, so round up: 6,000.

✓ To round a decimal number to a particular place, look at the digit in the **next** place to the right. If it is 4 or lower, round down. If it is 5 or higher, round up.

What is 5.345 rounded to the nearest hundredth?

Look at the digit in the thousandths place: 5.34**5**.

Since the digit is 5, round up: 5.35.

✓ To estimate using whole numbers, round any number that has more than one digit. Then perform the operation.

There were 324 mugs in a shop arranged on each of 8 shelves. How many mugs were on each shelf?

$$8\overline{)324} \text{ is about } 8\overline{)320} \quad \begin{array}{l} 40 \\ \underline{320} \end{array}$$

There were **about** 40 mugs on each shelf.

✓ Use estimation to decide if an answer is reasonable.

There were 584 paper clips in a box. Justin used 312 of the clips to make a chain. He believes there are 202 paper clips left. Is Justin's answer reasonable?

584 rounds up to 600 and 312 rounds down to 300. Subtract the rounded numbers: 600 − 300 = 300. So, no, 202 paper clips is **not** a reasonable answer. The actual answer would be closer to 300.

---

### Remember—

If the digit is—

0 1 2 3 4 | 5 6 7 8 9

← round down   round up →

When you round a number, replace any digit below the place you are rounding to with a zero.

150 → to the nearest ten, use a zero for the ones place

200 → to the nearest hundred, use zeros for the tens and ones places

The word *about* in a problem is a clue that the answer should be an estimate.

From left to right, the names of the places are:

| TEN THOUSANDS | THOUSANDS | HUNDREDS | TENS | ONES | DECIMAL POINT | TENTHS | HUNDREDTHS | THOUSANDTHS |
|---|---|---|---|---|---|---|---|---|
| 5 | 7, | 3 | 1 | 2 | . | 8 | 4 | 9 |

The symbol ≈ means "is about equal to."

**Read each problem. Circle the letter of the best answer.**

**1** A jar of jelly beans weighs 5.544 pounds. What is this number rounded to the nearest hundreth?

A   6.044          C   5.540

B   5.550          D   5.044

> The correct answer is C. To round 5.544 to the nearest hundreth, look at the number in the thousandths place: 5.54**4**. It is a 4, so round down: 5.540.

**2** Caleb spent $185 on food for a party. He spent $62 on decorations. He thinks the total he spent on food and decorations is *about* $300. Is his estimate reasonable?

A   Yes, the answer should be *about* $300.

B   No, the answer should be *about* $150.

C   No, the answer should be *about* $200.

D   No, the answer should be *about* $250.

**3** The waters of Lake Superior, one of the Great Lakes, reach a depth of 1,333 feet. What is this number rounded to the nearest hundred?

A   1,400          C   1,300

B   1,330          D   1,000

**4** Mike rounded 18.344 to 18.300. To which place did he round the number?

A   ones           C   hundredths

B   tenths         D   thousandths

**5** A new computer sells for $939. It is on sale for $775. Janine estimates that she'll save *about* $160 by buying it on sale. Is her estimate reasonable?

A   Yes, the answer should be *about* $160.

B   No, the answer should be *about* $140.

C   No, the answer should be *about* $150.

D   No, the answer should be *about* $200.

**6** Today, 6,973 letters are handled by the local post office. What is this number rounded to the nearest thousand?

A   6,000          C   7,000

B   6,900          D   7,900

**7** Mrs. Velez's car can travel 29 miles on a gallon of gasoline. Mrs. Velez estimates that she can travel 200 miles on 8 gallons of gasoline. Is her estimate reasonable?

A   Yes, the answer should be *about* $10 \times 20 = 200$.

B   No, the answer should be *about* $8 \times 20 = 160$.

C   No, the answer should be *about* $10 \times 30 = 300$.

D   No, the answer should be *about* $8 \times 30 = 240$.

**Unit 5** Estimation

**Read each problem. Write your answers.**

**8** Look at the number line below.

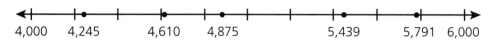

4,000  4,245    4,610    4,875       5,439     5,791  6,000

*Part A*

Which three numbers round to 5,000?

*Answer:* ____4,610____ and ____4,875____ and ____5,439____

*Part B*

Explain why your answer is correct.

> You are asked which numbers round to 5,000. To round to the thousands place, look at the numbers in the hundreds place. Numbers less than 5 round down, so 5,439 rounds to 5,000. Numbers greater than 5 round up, so 4,610 and 4,875 round up to 5,000.

**9** As of 2010, there were about 6,975 people living in a certain county. The county has an area of about 72 square miles.

*Part A*

Paul says there are **about** 96 people per square mile in the county. Is this answer reasonable?

*Answer:* _____

*Part B*

Use estimation to justify your answer.

_____

_____

_____

_____

**Unit 5** Estimation

**Read the problem. Write your answer for each part.**

10  Regular gasoline in one town costs $3.63 per gallon.

*Part A*

What is the price of gas per gallon rounded to the nearest dollar?

*Answer:* $_____

**Ask Yourself**
Which digit do I look at when rounding to the nearest whole number?

*Part B*

Quincy thinks it will cost $33.60 to fill his tank with 10 gallons of gas. Is Quincy's guess a reasonable estimation?

*Answer:* _____

*Part C*

Use estimation to justify your answer to Part B.

_____

_____

_____

_____

# Estimating with Fractions

**Indicators** 5.N.25, 27 **CCSS** 5.NF.2

✓ A fraction can be rounded to 0, $\frac{1}{2}$, or 1 by comparing the numerator and denominator.

If the numerator is much smaller than the denominator, round the fraction to 0.

$$\frac{1}{8} \qquad \frac{2}{7} \qquad \frac{5}{63}$$

If the denominator is about twice as large as the numerator, you can round the fraction to $\frac{1}{2}$.

$$\frac{5}{8} \qquad \frac{13}{25} \qquad \frac{45}{93}$$

If the numerator is nearly the same as the denominator, you can round the fraction to 1.

$$\frac{7}{8} \qquad \frac{11}{12} \qquad \frac{70}{72}$$

✓ To estimate sums and differences of fractions, first round the fraction to 0, $\frac{1}{2}$, or 1.

Mr. Gordon used $2\frac{3}{4}$ books of stamps to mail invitations. He used $1\frac{1}{5}$ books of stamps to send thank-you notes. He said he used **about** 4 books of stamps in all. Is this a reasonable estimate?

Round $\frac{3}{4}$ to 1. So $2\frac{3}{4}$ is **about** 3.

Round $\frac{1}{5}$ to 0. So $1\frac{1}{5}$ is **about** 1.

Add: $3 + 1 = 4$.

Mr. Gordon's estimate of **about** 4 books of stamps is reasonable.

**Remember—**

The numerator and denominator are the terms of a fraction.

$\frac{1}{8}$ ← Numerator
   ← Denominator

A fraction with the numerator equal to or greater than the denominator is called an improper fraction.

$$\frac{9}{4} = 2\frac{1}{4}$$

$$\frac{16}{6} = 2\frac{4}{6} = 2\frac{2}{3}$$

A mixed number is a whole number and a fraction.

To change a mixed number to an improper fraction, multiply the denominator by the whole number and add the numerator. The denominator stays the same.

$$5\frac{2}{7} = \frac{37}{7}$$

To add or subtract fractions with like denominators, simply add or subtract the numerators. The denominators stay the same.

**Unit 5** Estimation

**Read each problem. Circle the letter of the best answer.**

**1** What is the estimated sum of $\frac{10}{12} + \frac{7}{12}$?

A $\frac{1}{2}$        C $1\frac{1}{2}$

B 1        D 2

> The correct answer is C. In the fraction $\frac{10}{12}$, the numerator is nearly the same as the denominator, so it can be rounded to 1. In the fraction $\frac{7}{12}$, the denominator is about twice as large as the numerator, so it can be rounded to $\frac{1}{2}$. Then add the estimates: $1 + \frac{1}{2} = 1\frac{1}{2}$.

**2** Rianna lives $6\frac{7}{9}$ miles from Lake George. Griffin lives $3\frac{1}{9}$ miles from the lake. What is the **best** estimate of how much farther Rianna lives from Lake George than Griffin?

A 3 miles        C 5 miles

B 4 miles        D 6 miles

**3** Talik had three books. The books weighed $1\frac{1}{10}$ pounds, $2\frac{3}{10}$ pounds, and $1\frac{8}{10}$ pounds. Talik estimated that the total weight of the three books was $4\frac{1}{2}$ pounds. Is this estimate reasonable?

A Yes, it should be **about** $4\frac{1}{2}$ pounds.

B No, it should be **about** 5 pounds.

C No, it should be **about** $5\frac{1}{2}$ pounds.

D No, it should be **about** 6 pounds.

**4** Rosita rode her bike $1\frac{1}{8}$ miles on Monday, $2\frac{4}{8}$ miles on Tuesday, and $3\frac{6}{8}$ miles on Wednesday. What is the **best** estimate of the total distance she rode?

A $6\frac{1}{2}$ miles        C $7\frac{1}{2}$ miles

B 7 miles        D 8 miles

**5** What is the **best** estimate of $3\frac{6}{12} + 2\frac{10}{12}$?

A less than 5

B between 5 and $5\frac{1}{2}$

C between $5\frac{1}{2}$ and 6

D more than 6

**6** Mrs. Kim has a cactus that is $3\frac{8}{16}$ inches tall. A second cactus is $9\frac{11}{16}$ inches tall. She estimated the height of both plants at $13\frac{1}{2}$ inches. Is this reasonable?

A Yes, they are **about** $13\frac{1}{2}$ inches tall.

B No, they are **about** 14 inches tall.

C No, they are **about** $12\frac{1}{2}$ inches tall.

D No, they are **about** 12 inches tall.

**7** What is the **best** estimate of $9\frac{12}{25} - 6\frac{23}{25}$?

A 2        C 3

B $2\frac{1}{2}$        D $3\frac{1}{2}$

**Read each problem. Write your answers.**

**8** Jack bought a piece of paneling $8\frac{3}{7}$ feet long. He cut a piece $2\frac{5}{7}$ feet long from it. **About** how much paneling was left?

*Show your work.*

$$\frac{3}{7} \approx \frac{1}{2} \text{ so } 8\frac{3}{7} \approx 8\frac{1}{2}$$
$$\frac{5}{7} \approx 1 \text{ so } 2\frac{5}{7} \approx 2 + 1 = 3$$
$$8\frac{1}{2} - 3 = 5\frac{1}{2}$$

*Answer:* **about** _____ $5\frac{1}{2}$ _____ feet

First round each fraction to the nearest 0, $\frac{1}{2}$, or 1: $\frac{3}{7}$ is about $\frac{1}{2}$ and $\frac{5}{7}$ is about 1. Then subtract: $8\frac{1}{2} - 3 = 5\frac{1}{2}$.

**9** Chef Carson used $2\frac{5}{10}$ packages of pasta during lunch and $5\frac{4}{10}$ packages during dinner. He estimated that he used a total of 8 packages of pasta that day.

*Part A*

Is his estimate reasonable?

*Answer:* _____

*Part B*

Use estimation to justify your answer.

_____

_____

_____

_____

**Read the problem. Write your answer for each part.**

**10** The Cleary family had $8\frac{18}{20}$ acres of land. They cleared $1\frac{3}{20}$ acres to build a barn.

### Part A

Estimate the amount of land left.

*Show your work.*

**Ask Yourself**

Are the fractions close to $0$, $\frac{1}{2}$, or $1$?

*Answer:* _____ acres

### Part B

The section of land cleared was next to an open field $3\frac{8}{20}$ acres in size. The Cleary family estimated that the total open area is now 4 acres. Is this reasonable? Explain why or why not.

_____

_____

_____

# Estimating with Decimals

**Indicators** 5.N.26, 27

To estimate sums and differences with decimals, round to the nearest whole number. Then add or subtract the rounded numbers.

Felix's dog weighs 45.6 pounds. His cat weighs 11.3 pounds. Estimate how much the dog and cat weigh together.

$$45.6 \text{ rounds to } 46$$
$$+11.3 \text{ rounds to } 11$$

They weigh **about** 57 pounds.

One snake is 82.7 centimeters long. A second snake is 59.9 centimeters long. **About** how much shorter is the second snake than the first?

$$82.7 \text{ rounds to } 83$$
$$-59.9 \text{ rounds to } 60$$

It is **about** 23 centimeters shorter.

To estimate products and quotients, first round any number with more than one digit. Then multiply or divide the rounded numbers.

Reuben bought a T-shirt for $8.95. **About** how much would Reuben pay for 4 T-shirts?

$8.95 is **about** $9.
$4 \times \$9 = \$36$     Reuben would pay **about** $36.

Martha spent $53.70 for some T-shirts. **About** how many T-shirts did she buy?

$53.70 is **about** $54.
$8.95 is **about** $9.
$54 \div 9 = 6$     Martha bought **about** 6 T-shirts.

## Remember—

The word *about* in a problem is a clue that the answer should be an estimate.

To round a number to a certain place, look at the digit in the next place to the right. If it is 5, 6, 7, 8, or 9, round **up.**

Round 58 to the nearest ten. Look at the ones. **58** rounds up to 60.

If the digit is 4, 3, 2, or 1, round **down.**

Round 937 to the nearest hundred. Look at the tens. **9**3**7** rounds down to 900.

Sometimes you need to round a decimal number to a whole number. Other times you need to round it to the nearest tenth.

Round 5.35 to the nearest whole number. Look at the tenths.

5.35 rounds down to 5.0.

Round 5.35 to the nearest tenth. Look at the hundredths.

5.35 rounds up to 5.4.

**Read each problem. Circle the letter of the best answer.**

Use this table to answer questions 1–3.

The table shows the number of hours some people volunteered at an animal shelter last year.

**Volunteer Time**

| Name | Hours Worked |
|---|---|
| Kendon | 87.97 |
| Mahbub | 108.32 |
| Alexa | 98.43 |
| Camille | 105.50 |

**1** **About** how many more hours did Mahbub volunteer than Kendon?

A   18 hours     C   20 hours

B   19 hours     D   21 hours

> The correct answer is C. To estimate the difference, round the numbers: 108.32 rounds down to 108 and 87.97 rounds up to 88. Then subtract: 108 − 88 = 20.

**2** Which of these is the **best** estimate of the combined hours of Alexa and Camille?

A   201 hours     C   203 hours

B   202 hours     D   204 hours

**3** Alexa has volunteered the same number of hours for the last 5 years. She estimates that she worked a total of 500 hours for that time period. Is her estimate reasonable?

A   Yes, she worked **about** 500 hours.

B   No, she worked **about** 450 hours.

C   No, she worked **about** 475 hours.

D   No, she worked **about** 490 hours.

**4** A car traveled at an average speed of 57.36 miles per hour. If it traveled for 4.8 hours, **about** how far did it travel?

A   280 miles     C   290 miles

B   285 miles     D   295 miles

**5** Shawna bought 12 pounds of meat for a family reunion. The price of the meat was $2.85 per pound. She estimates she spent about $30 for the meat. Is her estimate reasonable?

A   Yes, the answer should be **about** $30.

B   No, the answer should be **about** $18.

C   No, the answer should be **about** $24.

D   No, the answer should be **about** $36.

**6** Ian has $20 to buy groceries. If he buys 4 cartons of milk, **about** how many pounds of chicken can he buy?

MILK $1.99     CHICKEN $1.79 per pound

A   2     C   6

B   4     D   8

**7** A group of 6 friends bought a wedding gift for $252.58. If they shared the cost equally, **about** how much money did each pay?

A   $42     C   $62

B   $52     D   $72

**Read each problem. Write your answers.**

8   The advertisement at the right shows the prices for shoes and sneakers at a local store.

SHOES
$45.50

SNEAKERS
$28.35

*Part A*

**About** how much would two pairs of shoes and one pair of sneakers cost?

*Show your work.*

$$\$45.50 \approx \$46$$
$$\$28.35 \approx \$28$$

$$\begin{array}{r} 46 \\ \times 2 \\ \hline \$92 \end{array}$$

$$\begin{array}{r} \$92 \\ +\$28 \\ \hline \$120 \end{array}$$

*Answer:* **about** $_____120_____

*Part B*

Explain your answer.

First round the shoe price of $45.50 to $46. Then multiply to find the price of two pairs of shoes: 2 × $46 = $92. Next, round the price of sneakers: $28.35 to $28. Finally, add the rounded prices: $92 + $28 = $120.

9   Harry's mom's car averages 25.19 miles per gallon. His dad's car averages 17.7 miles per gallon. Harry believes his mom's car gets 5.5 miles per gallon **more** than his dad's car.

*Part A*

Is Harry's answer reasonable?

*Answer:* _____

*Part B*

Use estimation to explain your answer.

_____

_____

_____

_____

**Read the problem. Write your answer for each part.**

**10** Bethpage State Park has five golf courses to challenge golfers of all skill levels.

### Part A

The Black Course is the toughest, with a difficulty rating of 76.6. The Green Course has a rating of 69.5. Tamika said the difference in ratings is 7. Is her answer reasonable?

*Ask Yourself*
What numbers do the ratings round to?

*Answer:* _____

### Part B

Use estimation to justify your answer.

_____

_____

_____

_____

### Part C

Last summer, Olivia played the Red Course. It has a rating of 72.2. **About** how much higher is the Black Course rating than the Red Course rating?

*Show your work.*

*Answer:* _____

# Estimation Review

**Read each problem. Circle the letter of the best answer.**

**1** When rounded to the nearest thousand, which of these numbers does **not** round to 5,000?

  A  4,500          C  5,137

  B  4,623          D  5,551

**2** Which is the **best** estimate of the difference of $9\frac{6}{7} - 3\frac{1}{7}$?

  A  4              C  6

  B  5              D  7

**3** If Pete buys 4 loaves of bread, **about** how much will he spend?

  BREAD
  $1.89

  A  $5            C  $7

  B  $6            D  $8

**4** What is 6.078 rounded to the nearest hundredth?

  A  6.06          C  6.08

  B  6.07          D  6.09

**5** Which of these is the **best** estimate of $4\frac{13}{24} + 5\frac{21}{24}$?

  A  9             C  10

  B  $9\frac{1}{2}$         D  $10\frac{1}{2}$

**6** One rabbit has a length of 41.2 centimeters. Another has a length of 43.6 centimeters. What is the **best** estimate of the difference in their lengths?

  A  1 centimeter    C  3 centimeters

  B  2 centimeters    D  4 centimeters

**7** Sandy bought 2 pizzas at $10.95 each and 5 bottles of soda at $2.09 each. Which of the following is the **best** estimate of the total cost?

  A  $30           C  $34

  B  $32           D  $36

**8** A strip of wood is 8.67 inches long. Melanie used 5 of them for a model project. She says the total length of the strips of wood is 45.55 inches. Is this answer reasonable?

  A  Yes, the answer should be **about** $9 \times 5 = 45$.

  B  No, the answer should be **about** $8 \times 5 = 40$.

  C  No, the answer should be **about** $9 \times 6 = 54$.

  D  No, the answer should be **about** $8 \times 6 = 48$.

**Read each problem. Write your answers.**

**9** Arie recorded the rainfall for the last three months in his town. Estimate the total rainfall for the three months.

**Show your work.**

| CATESVILLE RAINFALL | |
|---|---|
| **Month** | **Rainfall (in inches)** |
| December | $3\frac{1}{10}$ |
| January | $7\frac{5}{10}$ |
| February | $9\frac{8}{10}$ |

**Answer: about** _____ inches

**10** The Jamaica Bay Wildlife Refuge is the home to many different birds.

*Part A*

A 1.75-mile trail circles one of the ponds in the refuge. If Aaron visits the refuge 5 times and completes the trail each time, **about** how many miles will he have hiked?

**Answer: about** _____ miles

*Part B*

A second trail is 2.15 miles long. **About** how long are both trails?

**Answer: about** _____ miles

**11** The table at the right shows the average attendance at the last four baseball games of the Jefferson City Jets.

*Part A*

Which two dates had the same attendance when rounded to the nearest thousand?

**Answer:** _____ and _____

| BASEBALL ATTENDANCE | |
|---|---|
| **Date** | **Attendance** |
| 6/05 | 14,459 |
| 6/11 | 15,389 |
| 6/13 | 15,839 |
| 6/16 | 16,398 |

*Part B*

Explain why your answer is correct.

_____

_____

_____

**Read the problem. Write your answer for each part.**

**12** This sign hangs above the entrance to Howe's Caverns.

> **Howe's Caverns Admissions**
>
> Adults: $18
>
> Children: $9
>
> School Discounts for Groups of 15 or More Children: $7.88

*Part A*

**About** how much will a class of 20 children save by paying the discount price?

*Show your work.*

*Answer: **about** $_____*

*Part B*

Explain how you found your answer.

_____

_____

_____

*Part C*

For groups of 15 or more adults, there is a $6 savings from the regular admission price of $18. Georgetta believes a group of 65 adults will save $300 with the group rate. Is her answer reasonable? Use estimation to justify your answer.

_____

_____

_____

Unit 5 Estimation

# Unit 6
## Algebra

You use algebra to show mathematical relationships. You can write expressions and equations to describe real-life situations. Sometimes a value is unknown or can change, so you use a variable to represent that value. You can also use algebra to show the rule for a number or geometric pattern. This unit will help you understand expressions, equations, and patterns.

Lesson 1 **Variables and Expressions** reviews how to write an expression to describe a situation. You will also review the meaning of variables and constants.

Lesson 2 **Evaluating Expressions** reviews how to find the value of an expression when given the value of a variable.

Lesson 3 **Solving Equations** reviews how to find the value of an equation by isolating the variable.

Lesson 4 **Numeric and Geometric Patterns** reviews how to describe the rule of a pattern as an algebraic expression. You will also find missing numbers or shapes in patterns.

# Variables and Expressions

**Indicators** 5.A.1, 2 **CCSS** 5.OA.2

 An **expression** is a name for a number.

$$7 \qquad 5 + 3 \qquad \frac{10}{2} \qquad n \times 3$$

An expression can be only a number, or it can contain numbers, letters, and operations. A letter that stands for a number that can change is called a **variable.** An expression containing a variable is an **algebraic expression.**

There are 4 more SUVs than cars in a parking lot. If $n$ is the number of cars, what is the number of SUVs?

The number of SUVs can be expressed as $n + 4$.

 A verbal expression can be translated into an algebraic expression.

| | |
|---|---|
| $n + 5$ | Five more than a number |
| $n - 5$ | Five less than a number |
| $3n$ | Three times a number |
| $\frac{n}{3}$ | A number divided by three |
| $3n + 5$ | Five more than three times a number |

## Remember—

The letters $n$, $x$, and $y$ are often used for variables, but a variable can be any letter.

The multiplication sign, $\times$, can be confused with the variable $x$. So some multiplication expressions do not use $\times$ for multiplication. If a letter and number are side by side, it means multiplication.

$2n$ is the same as $2 \times n$.

Addition, subtraction, multiplication, and division are operations.

Some words give clues about operations.

*Divided among* or *split equally* signals division.

*Total, in all,* or *altogether* may signal addition or multiplication.

*Less than* or *difference* usually signals subtraction.

A **constant** is a number that does not change.

$d$ = the number of hours in a day

In this case, $d$ always equals 24, so it is a constant.

**Unit 6** Algebra

**Read each problem. Circle the letter of the best answer.**

**1** Bernice earns $m$ dollars per day. Her friend, Jorge, earns three times as much. Which expression shows the amount Jorge earns?

**A** $m + 3$      **C** $m - 3$

**B** $m \div 3$      **D** $3 \times m$

> The correct answer is D. If Jorge earns "three times as much" as Bernice, this is represented by the expression $3m$, which is the same as $3 \times m$.

**2** This expression shows that an antique dealer doubles the price of an object and subtracts $5 to get the selling price.

$$2c - 5$$

Which word describes the letter $c$?

**A** constant      **C** operation

**B** variable      **D** product

**3** In February, there were 100 fewer customers in a restaurant than in March. If $r$ represents the number of customers in March, which expression represents the number of customers in February?

**A** $r - 100$      **C** $r + 100$

**B** $r \div 100$      **D** $r \times 100$

**4** What could this expression represent?

$$c + 15$$

**A** 15 less than a number

**B** 15 times a number

**C** 15 more than a number

**D** 15 divided by a number

**5** The Battle of Saratoga was fought $m$ years before the surrender of the British at Yorktown in 1781. Which expression can be used to represent the year the Battle of Saratoga was fought?

**A** $m - 1781$

**B** $1781 + m$

**C** $1781 - m$

**D** $1781 \times m$

**6** Look at this expression.

$$n - 1 + 8$$

Which situation could this expression represent?

**A** Don has some pencils. He gave 1 to Linda and bought 8 more pencils.

**B** Don has some pencils. He gave 8 to Linda and bought 1 more pencil.

**C** Don has 8 pencils. He gave 1 to Linda and bought some more pencils.

**D** Don has 1 pencil. He gave some to Linda and bought 8 more pencils.

**7** Which describes a constant?

**A** the number of days of vacation

**B** the number of days in a week

**C** the price of a school lunch

**D** the price of a gallon of gasoline

**Unit 6** Algebra

103

**Read each problem. Write your answers.**

**8** The area of Lake Superior is $n$ square miles. Lake Victoria in Africa is 4,872 square miles smaller than Lake Superior.

**Part A**

Write an expression to represent the area in square miles of Lake Victoria.

*Answer:* _____ $n - 4,872$ _____

**Part B**

Explain how you know your answer is correct.

> The variable $n$ represents the area of Lake Superior. Lake Victoria is smaller than Lake Superior. Its area is 4,872 square miles *less* than Superior. So, Lake Victoria's area can be expressed as $n - 4,872$.

**9** Tina is $n$ years younger than Marvin. Marvin is 15. The expression $15 - n$ represents Tina's age.

**Part A**

Is $n$ a constant or a variable here? How do you know?

_____

_____

_____

**Part B**

Tina is $\frac{1}{3}$ Jon's age, $m$. The expression $\frac{m}{3}$ represents Tina's age. Is $m$ a constant or a variable here? Explain your answer.

_____

_____

_____

Unit 6 Algebra

**Read the problem. Write your answer for each part.**

**10** The Old Croton Trailway is located *m* miles from the Hudson River Museum. Just 6.2 miles north of the trailway is Sunnyside, the home of the author Washington Irving.

**Part A**

What does *m* represent?

_____

_____

**Part B**

Write an expression to represent the distance from the Hudson River Museum to Sunnyside, going through the Old Croton Trailway.

*Answer:* _____

> ***Ask Yourself***
> What operation do I use to find the total distance?

**Part C**

The Tappan Zee Bridge crosses the Hudson River one mile north of Sunnyside. Write an expression to represent the distance from the Old Croton Trailway to the Tappan Zee Bridge.

*Answer:* _____

To **evaluate** an expression means to find its value. You can do this by substituting a given number for the variable and then performing the operation.

> Jacinto had 23 books. He bought some more books at a sale. If $b$ is the number of books he bought, what is the total number of books he now has?
>
> The total number of books can be expressed as $23 + b$.
>
> If Jacinto bought 6 more books, how many books did he have in all?
>
> Substitute 6 for $b$ in the expression.
>
> $$23 + b \rightarrow 23 + 6$$
>
> Then do the addition.
>
> $$23 + 6 = 29$$
>
> Jacinto has 29 books in all.

When an expression contains more than one operation, complete the operations using the **order of operations.**

> What is the value of $(3 + 2) \times 8 - b$ if $b = 5$?

First substitute the given value for the variable.

$$(3 + 2) \times 8 - 5$$

Then carry out the operations, following the order of operations.

Parentheses:   $(3 + 2) \times 8 - 5$
              $5 \times 8 - 5$

Multiplication:   $5 \times 8 - 5$
               $40 - 5$

Subtraction:   $40 - 5$
            $35$

### Remember—

An **expression** can contain numbers, letters, and operations.

A letter that stands for a number that can change is called a **variable.**

Addition, subtraction, multiplication, and division are operations.

Some words give clues about operations.

*Total, in all,* or *altogether* may signal addition or multiplication.

*Divided among* or *split equally* signals division.

*Less than* or *difference* usually signals subtraction.

The order of operations is parentheses, multiplication or division in order from left to right, then addition or subtraction in order from left to right.

**Read each problem. Circle the letter of the best answer.**

**1** What is the value of the following expression if $n = 10$?

$$3 + (n \times 5)$$

**A** 5

**B** 8

**C** 18

**D** 53

> The correct answer is D. First substitute 10 for the variable $n$: $3 + (10 \times 5)$. Then do the operations in parentheses: $10 \times 5 = 50$. Finally, add: $3 + 50 = 53$. The product is 53.

**2** What is the value of the expression $4z$, if $z = 8$?

**A** 2

**B** 4

**C** 32

**D** 48

**3** There are 52 weeks in a year. The expression below names the number of weeks remaining in the year if $w$ weeks have passed.

$$52 - w$$

Evaluate the expression if $w = 13$.

**A** 4

**B** 39

**C** 65

**D** 100

**4** What is the value of the expression $75 + c$, if $c = 3$?

**A** 25

**C** 78

**B** 72

**D** 225

**5** Which of these expressions will **not** result in a value of 5 if $a = 8$?

**A** $(a + 7) \div 3$

**C** $(33 - a) \div 5$

**B** $(a \div 2) + 1$

**D** $(a \times 2) - 8$

**6** It snowed 10 days in January for a total of $n$ inches of snow. The expression below shows the average snow fall per day over the 10 days.

$$\frac{n}{10}$$

Evaluate the expression if $n = 20$.

**A** 2 inches

**C** 30 inches

**B** 10 inches

**D** 200 inches

**7** Trena made a number of beaded necklaces, $b$. She sold 15 of the necklaces. She wanted to share the rest of the necklaces with her friends. She wrote the expression below to show how many necklaces each person would get if she shared them with three friends.

$$\frac{(b - 15)}{3}$$

Evaluate the expression if $b = 90$.

**A** 25

**C** 90

**B** 35

**D** 225

**Read each problem. Write your answers.**

**8** Prakash baked a certain number of cupcakes, *n*. He packed them in 2 boxes. He used the expression $\frac{n}{2}$ to show how many cupcakes went in each box.

*Part A*

What is the value of the expression if *n* = 18?

*Show your work.*

$$\frac{18}{2} = 2\overline{)18} \quad \begin{array}{r} 9 \\ \hline 18 \\ \underline{18} \end{array}$$

*Answer:* _____9_____ cupcakes

*Part B*

How would the value of the expression change if *n* = 30? Explain.

> To evaluate the expression, substitute the given value in the expression and carry out the operation: 18 ÷ 2 = 9. To find how the value changes in Part B, first substitute 30 for *n*: 30 ÷ 2 = 15. Then subtract the quotient from the answer to Part A: 15 − 9 = 6. The value of the expression would increase by 6.

**9** The area that is now Pennsylvania became a British colony in 1681. The area that is now New York became a colony *b* years before Pennsylvania.

*Part A*

Write an expression which represents the year New York became a colony.

*Answer:* _____

*Part B*

Evaluate the expression you wrote for Part A if the value of *b* is 17.

*Show your work.*

*Answer:* _____

**Read the problem. Write your answer for each part.**

**10** Look at this expression.

$$\frac{(9 + n) \times 4}{3}$$

**Part A**

Evaluate this expression if $n = 6$.

**Show your work.**

*Ask Yourself*
What operation
must I do first?

Answer: _____

**Part B**

What is the value of the expression if the parentheses are removed?

**Show your work.**

Answer: _____

# Solving Equations

**Indicators  5.A.4, 5**

✔ An **equation** is a number sentence that says two things are equal. Both sides of the equation are in balance.

$$18 - 9 = 3 \times 3$$

$$18 - 9 = 9 \text{ and } 3 \times 3 = 9$$

So $18 - 9 = 3 \times 3$ because $9 = 9$.

A box or letter can stand for a missing number in an equation.

Joe weighs 97 pounds. He and his sister together weigh 167 pounds. How much does Joe's sister weigh?

$$97 + w = 167$$

✔ To solve the equation, "undo" the operation by using the opposite, or inverse, operation. Rewrite the equation to isolate the variable on one side.

$$97 + w = 167$$

To isolate $w$, subtract 97 from **both** sides.

$$97 - 97 + w = 167 - 97$$
$$w = 70$$

Joe's sister weighs 70 pounds.

---

**Remember—**

If the sides of an equation do not balance, the equation is **not** true.

$$5 + 9 \stackrel{?}{=} 6 \times 3$$
$$14 \neq 18$$

Because 14 does not equal 18, $5 + 9$ does not equal $6 \times 3$.

**Isolate** means "to set apart."

Addition and subtraction are inverse operations. You can add to check subtraction or subtract to check addition.

$$21 - 9 = 12$$
$$\text{because}$$
$$9 + 12 = 21$$

Multiplication and division are also inverse operations. You can multiply to check division or divide to check multiplication.

$$42 \div 7 = 6$$
$$\text{because}$$
$$6 \times 7 = 42$$

To keep an equation in balance, perform the same operation on **both** sides.

**Read each problem. Circle the letter of the best answer.**

**1** What is the value of $q$ in this equation?

$$q \div 5 = 10$$

**A** 2

**B** 5

**C** 15

**D** 50

> The correct answer is D. To isolate the variable, use the inverse operation of division, multiplication. Multiply each side by 5: $5 \times q \div 5 = 10 \times 5$. So $q = 50$.

**2** The Statue of Liberty celebrated its 100th anniversary in 1986. The United Nations opened 41 years before the anniversary. The equation below represents the year the United Nations opened.

$$n + 41 = 1986$$

How is this equation solved?

**A** add 41 and 1986

**B** subtract 41 from 1986

**C** multiply 41 and 1986

**D** divide 1986 by 41

**3** Look at this equation.

$$6 \times a = 36$$

What value of $a$ makes this equation true?

**A** 6

**B** 30

**C** 42

**D** 216

**4** Tremaine had $d$ dollars. He spent $7 on lunch, and had $11 left. He showed this by the equation $d - \$7 = \$11$. How is this equation solved?

**A** add 11 and 7

**B** subtract 7 from 11

**C** multiply 7 by 11

**D** divide 11 by 7

**5** What is the solution for the equation $g \times 20 = 80$?

**A** $g = 3$

**B** $g = 4$

**C** $g = 5$

**D** $g = 6$

**6** How would the equation $z \times 12 = 36$ be solved?

**A** subtract 12 from 36

**B** multiply 36 by 12

**C** divide 36 by 12

**D** add 12 and 36

**7** A board game cost $12. The board game and game cartridge together cost $28. This is represented by the equation $\$12 + n = \$28$. How much did the game cartridge cost?

**A** $3

**B** $16

**C** $40

**D** $336

**Unit 6** Algebra

**Read each problem. Write your answers.**

**8** Look at this equation.

$$8n = 448$$

**Part A**

Solve the equation for $n$.

*Answer:* _____ $n = 56$ _____

**Part B**

Explain why your answer is correct.

> To isolate the variable, use the inverse operation of multiplication—division. Divide each side by 8: $8 \times n \div 8 = 448 \div 8$. So $n = 56$.

**9** Look at these two equations.

$$5 + a = 8 \qquad 9 - a = 6$$

Does the variable have the same value in both equations?

*Show your work.*

*Answer:* _____

**Read the problem. Write your answer for each part.**

**10** Clarence scored 12 points in a basketball game. Clarence and Ed together scored 27 points.

### Part A

How many points did Ed score? Write and solve a number sentence. Let *e* stand for the number of points Ed scored.

***Show your work.***

**Ask Yourself**
How many points did Clarence and Ed score together? How many points did Clarence and Ed each score?

*Answer:* _____ points

### Part B

Ed and Pedro together scored 25 points. How many points did Pedro score? Explain how you found your answer.

_____

_____

_____

_____

# Numeric and Geometric Patterns

**Indicators 5.A.7, 8**

To find a **pattern** in a sequence of numbers, look at the numbers in order and decide how they change. The change can be described by a **rule.**

What number comes next in this pattern?

3, 6, 12, 24, 48, ___?___

Each number is 2 times the previous number:

$2 \times 3 = 6, 2 \times 6 = 12, 2 \times 12 = 24, 2 \times 24 = 48$

The rule for this pattern is "multiply by 2." To find the next number, multiply the last number by 2:

$2 \times 48 = 96$

The next number will be 96.

A pattern rule can be expressed algebraically. The pattern "multiply by 2" is the same as $2n$ or $2 \times n$.

To find a geometric pattern in a sequence of figures, look at the shapes. Find where the shapes or the position of a shape repeats.

The figures repeat themselves after three figures. The next figure in the geometric pattern would be ⊡.

Any operation can be used to change numbers in a pattern.

3, 5, 7, 9, 11, …
The rule is "add 2" or "$n + 2$."

24, 20, 16, 12, 8, …
The rule is "subtract 4" or "$n - 4$."

5, 25, 125, 625, …
The rule is "multiply by 5" or "$5m$."

120, 60, 30, 15, …
The rule is "divide by 2" or "$n \div 2$."

A geometric pattern can have two, three, or more elements before they repeat.

ABABABAB…

ABBABB…

ABCABC…

Sometimes a pattern uses a shape or picture that changes direction.

← ↑ → ↓ ← ↑ → ↓ ← ?

The arrows go left, up, right, down, and repeat. The last arrow points left, so the next one should point up, ↑.

**Read each problem. Circle the letter of the best answer.**

**1** Look at the number pattern shown below.

1, 3, 9, 27, …

Which algebraic expression names the rule for the pattern?

**A** $n \div 3$　　　**C** $3 \times n$

**B** $n + 3$　　　**D** $9 \times n$

> The correct answer is C. Each number in the sequence is multiplied by 3 to produce the next number: $3 \times 1 = \mathbf{3}$, $3 \times 3 = \mathbf{9}$, and $3 \times 9 = \mathbf{27}$. So whatever the number $n$, the expression gives you the next number. The rule is $3 \times n$.

**2** Isaac drew the pattern shown below.

What will the 25th block look like?

**A** 　　　**C**

**B** 　　　**D**

**3** Look at this function table.

| IN | OUT |
|----|-----|
| 18 | 6 |
| 21 | 7 |
| 12 | 4 |

If $n$ is the IN number, which algebraic expression names the rule for the OUT numbers?

**A** $n - 8$　　　**C** $n \times 3$

**B** $n \div 3$　　　**D** $n + 12$

**4** Look at the pattern below.

What is the missing shape?

**A** ○　　　**C** ▭

**B** △　　　**D** ▯

**5** Look at the pattern below.

3, 8, __?__, 18

Which algebraic expression names the rule for the pattern?

**A** $5n$　　　**C** $n + 5$

**B** $n \div 8$　　　**D** $18 - n$

**6** Chloe made the rule "$2n + 4$." If she starts with the number 4, what will be the next number in the pattern?

**A** 12

**B** 14

**C** 10

**D** 16

**7** If the pattern continues, how many □ will be in the next figure?

□　　□□□□　　□□□□□□□

**A** 9

**B** 10

**C** 11

**D** 12

**Read each problem. Write your answers.**

**8** Look at this pattern.

$$1, 3, 7, 15, \underline{\ ?\ }, \underline{\ ?\ } \ldots$$

*Part A*

Write an algebraic expression to represent the rule for the pattern.

*Answer:* _____ $2n + 1$ _____

*Part B*

What are the next two numbers in the pattern?

*Answer:* _____ 31 _____ and _____ 63 _____

> The pattern can be described algebraically as $2n + 1$. Use this rule to find the next two numbers. Substitute the last number for $n$ in the expression: $2(15) + 1 = 31$. Repeat with this number to find the next number: $2(31) + 1 = 63$.

**9** Look at this pattern.

*Part A*

Draw the missing figure from the pattern above.

*Part B*

Explain why your answer is correct.

_____

_____

_____

**Unit 6** Algebra

**Read the problem. Write your answer for each part.**

**10**  A marathon is a long race of 26.2 miles. Runners start training months before the race to get ready.

### Part A

Catrina started training by running $n$ miles per week. She increased her mileage by 2 miles each week. What is an algebraic expression that names the pattern?

*Ask Yourself*
What is the rule for the increase?

*Answer:* _____

### Part B

If Catrina started with 5 miles, how many miles did she run the sixth week?

**Show your work.**

*Answer:* _____ miles

### Part C

How many weeks will it take Catrina to reach 26 miles? Explain your answer.

_____

_____

_____

**Read each problem. Circle the letter of the best answer.**

**1** Look at this pattern.

What will be the next pattern in the figure?

A

C

B

D

**2** What is the value of the expression $(s - 20) \times 2$, when $s = 42$?

A 2          C 20

B 11         D 44

**3** Look at the number pattern below.

88, 44, 22, 11

Which algebraic expression names the rule for the pattern?

A $n \times 2$          C $n \div 4$

B $n \times 4$          D $n \div 2$

**4** Which describes a constant?

A the number of ounces in a pound

B the number of inches on a ruler

C the number of days in a month

D the number of apples in a bushel

**5** Which expression represents the sum of $b$ and 50?

A $b + 50$          C $50 \times b$

B $50 - b$          D $50 \div b$

**6** The location of Central Park was chosen 25 years before it opened in 1876. The year the location was chosen is represented by the equation shown below.

$$x + 25 = 1876$$

What year was the location for the park selected?

A 1848          C 1850

B 1849          D 1851

**7** How would the equation $d - \$25 = \$18$ be solved?

A subtract $18 from $25

B multiply $18 by $25

C add $25 and $18

D divide $25 by $18

**8** Look at the number pattern shown below.

1, 6, 36, __?__, 1,296

Which algebraic expression names the rule for the pattern?

A $n + 5$          C $n \div 6$

B $n \times 3$          D $n \times 6$

**Read each problem. Write your answers.**

**9** Last year, every 2 days, 50 new customers signed up for digital cable television. Every 4 days, 100 new customers signed up, and every 6 days, there were 150 new customers.

**Part A**

Write an algebraic expression to describe the rule for this pattern.

*Answer:* _____

**Part B**

If the pattern continues, how many customers will sign up every 10 days?

*Answer:* _____ customers

**10** Look at this equation.

$$5 \times n = 225$$

Solve the equation for *n*.

**Show your work.**

*Answer:* _____

**11** A ticket to a concert, *c*, costs $5 less than a ticket to a play.

**Part A**

Write an expression to represent the cost of a ticket to the play.

*Answer:* _____

**Part B**

What is the cost of a ticket to the play if a ticket to the concert is $60?

*Answer:* $_____

**Read the problem. Write your answer for each part.**

**12** The Underground Railroad was used to lead slaves to freedom during the Civil War.

### Part A

Harriet Tubman made about 20 trips on the Underground Railroad. If she led a total of $n$ people, write an expression to show the average number of slaves she led on each trip.

*Answer:* _____

### Part B

The total number of people, $p$, led through the Underground Railroad to the North is far greater than the number led by Harriet Tubman. It is represented by the equation shown below.

$$p + 10{,}000 = 60{,}000$$

How many people were led through the Underground Railroad in total?

***Show your work.***

*Answer:* _____ people

### Part C

Explain why your answer is correct.

_____

_____

_____

_____

# Unit 7
## Geometry, Part 1

In geometry, you study shapes. Shapes are made up of lines and angles. In order to understand the shapes, you must be able to identify different kinds of lines and angles. Shapes are named based on their sides and their angles they have. Squares and trapezoids are both types of quadrilaterals, but they look very different. Triangles can be classified by their sides and their angles. This lesson will help you understand lines, angles, quadrilaterals, and triangles.

Lesson 1 **Lines** reviews parallel, perpendicular, and intersecting lines. You will identify and draw these kinds of lines.

Lesson 2 **Angles** reviews how to identify acute, obtuse, and right angles. You will also measure and draw angles using a protractor.

Lesson 3 **Quadrilaterals** reviews how to identify different types of four-sided polygons. You will also find the measure of a missing angle in a quadrilateral.

Lesson 4 **Triangles** reviews how to identify triangles based on their angles and based on their sides. You will also find the measure of a third angle when you know the measures of the other two angles in a triangle.

# Lines

**Indicator   4.G.6**

## Remember—

✓ **Parallel lines** are always the same distance apart.

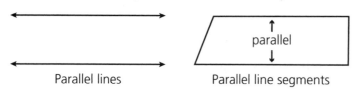

Parallel lines       Parallel line segments

A **line** has no endpoints. It is named by any two points on it.

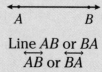

Line $AB$ or $BA$
$\overleftrightarrow{AB}$ or $\overleftrightarrow{BA}$

Parallel lines never meet. Line segments and rays can also be parallel.

✓ **Intersecting lines** meet or cross.

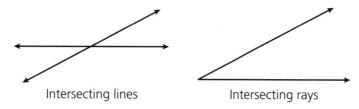

Intersecting lines       Intersecting rays

A **ray** has one endpoint. The endpoint is **always** named first.

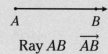

Ray $AB$   $\overrightarrow{AB}$

Intersecting lines create angles. Line segments and rays can also intersect.

A **line segment** has two endpoints. It is named by the endpoints.

Line segment $AB$ or $BA$
$\overline{AB}$ or $\overline{BA}$

✓ **Perpendicular lines** intersect at right angles.

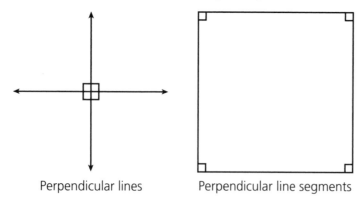

Perpendicular lines       Perpendicular line segments

Line segments and rays can also be perpendicular.

The point where lines, line segments, or rays meet is called a **vertex.**

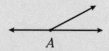

Point $A$ is a vertex.

A **right angle** is a square corner and measures 90°. The small square corner on a geometric figure means that angle is 90°.

**Unit 7** Geometry, Part 1

**Read each problem. Circle the letter of the best answer.**

**1** Which statement about parallel lines is true?

- **A** They intersect at right angles.
- **B** They can form two sides of a triangle.
- **C** They are always the same length.
- **D** They are always the same distance apart.

The correct answer is D. Parallel lines *never* intersect and are *always* the same distance apart.

**2** Which two lines below appear to be perpendicular?

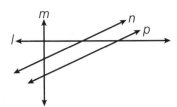

- **A** *l* and *m*
- **C** *m* and *n*
- **B** *l* and *p*
- **D** *n* and *p*

**3** This map shows four railroad tracks.

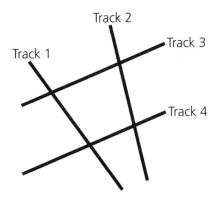

Which two tracks appear to be parallel?

- **A** 1 and 2
- **C** 2 and 4
- **B** 1 and 3
- **D** 3 and 4

**4** Which picture shows two intersecting lines that do **not** appear to be perpendicular?

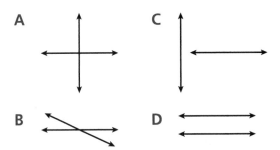

Use this map to answer questions 5 and 6.

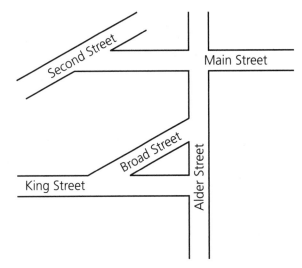

**5** Which street on this map appears to be parallel to Main Street?

- **A** Alder Street
- **C** King Street
- **B** Broad Street
- **D** Second Street

**6** Which statement about the map is true?

- **A** Main and Alder Streets appear perpendicular.
- **B** Broad and Second Streets appear perpendicular.
- **C** King Street appears to intersect Main Street.
- **D** Second and Alder Streets appear parallel.

**Read each problem. Write your answers.**

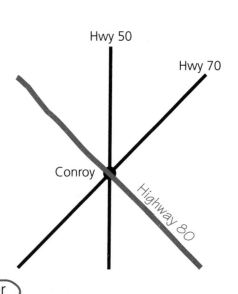

**7** The map shows two highways and the town of Conroy.

*Part A*

Highway 80 goes through Conroy, and it is perpendicular to Highway 70. On the map to the right, draw Highway 80.

*Part B*

Circle the choice below that **best** describes the relationship of Highway 80 and Highway 50.

parallel     perpendicular     (intersecting but not perpendicular)

If Highway 80 is perpendicular to Highway 70, then it crosses Highway 70 at a right angle. Draw a line at right angles to Highway 70 at Conroy, the point of intersection. Highway 50 and Highway 80 intersect at Conroy, but they do not form right angles.

**8** The map shows a road that is perpendicular to a canal. Goose Road is not shown. It is parallel to Heron Road.

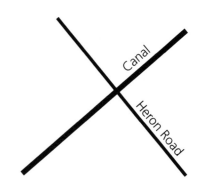

*Part A*

Draw and label Goose Road on the map to the right. What is the relationship of Goose Road and the canal?

*Answer:* _____

*Part B*

Explain how you know the relationship of Goose Road and the canal.

_____

_____

_____

_____

**Read the problem. Write your answer for each part.**

**9** ⊞ Use your ruler to help you solve this problem.

Walter drew two line segments. Line segment *AB* was 4 centimeters long. Line segment *BC* intersected and was perpendicular to line segment *AB*. It was 3 centimeters long.

### Part A

In the space below, draw and label Walter's figure.

> *Ask Yourself*
> What angle do perpendicular lines form?

### Part B

Explain why your drawing is correct.

_____

_____

_____

_____

### Part C

Suppose Walter drew a third line segment that intersected points *A* and *C*. Would this line segment be perpendicular or parallel to either $\overline{AB}$ or $\overline{BC}$? Explain your answer.

_____

_____

_____

_____

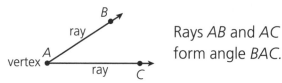

# Angles

**Indicators   4.G.7, 8; 5.M.6, 8**

✓ An **angle** is formed by two rays with a common endpoint. The point where they meet is called the **vertex** of the angle.

Rays *AB* and *AC* form angle *BAC*.

Lines and line segments also form angles when they intersect.

✓ Angles are measured in units called **degrees.** A **protractor** is a tool used to measure angles. A protractor is marked in degrees (°) from 0° to 180°. A protractor has two scales, one that reads from left to right and the other that reads from right to left. Every 10 degrees is marked with a number. Between the numbers are marks that stand for 1 degree.

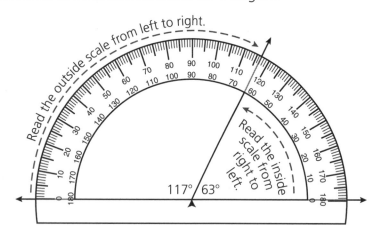

To use a protractor, line up the vertex of the angle with the mark at the center bottom of the protractor. Line up one ray with 0° on either end. Then read from 0 to the number the other ray passes through. *Be sure to read the same scale that the 0 you are starting from is on.*

---

### Remember—

A **ray** is named by its endpoint and one other point on the ray. The endpoint is **always** named first.

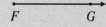

Ray *FG* **not** ray *GF*

An angle can be named three ways:

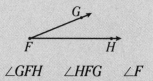

∠*GFH*   ∠*HFG*   ∠*F*

The symbol ∠ stands for "angle." The vertex is **always** named in the middle.

An **acute angle** measures less than 90°.

A **right angle** measures exactly 90°.

An **obtuse angle** measures more than 90° and less than 180°.

A **straight angle** measures 180°.

---

**Unit 7** Geometry, Part 1

**Read each problem. Circle the letter of the best answer.**

**1** 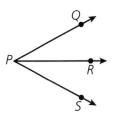 Use your protractor to help you solve this problem.

What is the measure of this angle, to the nearest degree?

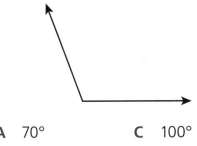

| | |
|---|---|
| **A** 70° | **C** 100° |
| **B** 80° | **D** 110° |

The correct answer is D. Line up the mark at the center bottom of the protractor with the vertex of the angle. Line up one ray with 0°. Then read from 0° to the number the other ray passes through. It measures 110°.

**2** Which angle in this figure appears to be acute?

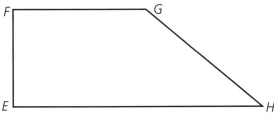

| | |
|---|---|
| **A** angle *E* | **C** angle *G* |
| **B** angle *F* | **D** angle *H* |

**3** Which tool would be **best** to measure angles on an architect's drawing?

**A** ruler

**B** scale

**C** protractor

**D** thermometer

**4** In the diagram below, which two rays are contained in angle *QPR*?

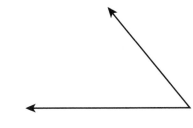

| | |
|---|---|
| **A** $\overrightarrow{PQ}$ and $\overrightarrow{PR}$ | **C** $\overrightarrow{QP}$ and $\overrightarrow{QR}$ |
| **B** $\overrightarrow{PQ}$ and $\overrightarrow{PS}$ | **D** $\overrightarrow{QP}$ and $\overrightarrow{QS}$ |

**5** 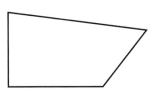 Use your protractor to help you solve this problem.

What is the measure of this angle to the nearest degree?

| | |
|---|---|
| **A** 40° | **C** 130° |
| **B** 50° | **D** 140° |

**6** Which describes the angles in this figure?

**A** 2 right angles, 2 acute angles

**B** 2 right angles, 1 acute angle, 1 obtuse angle

**C** 1 right angle, 2 acute angles, 1 obtuse angle

**D** 1 right angle, 1 acute angle, 2 obtuse angles

**Read each problem. Write your answers.**

**7** 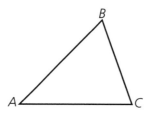 Use your protractor to help you solve this problem.

Kimberly drew this triangle.

**Part A**

How many degrees smaller is angle *A* than angle *B*?

*Answer:* _____20_____ °

**Part B**

Explain how you found your answer.

> Use the protractor to measure angles *A* and *B*. Angle *A* measures 45°, and angle *B* measures 65°. Then subtract: 65° − 45° = 20°.

**8** Use your protractor to help you solve this problem.

Look at the map of the United States below.

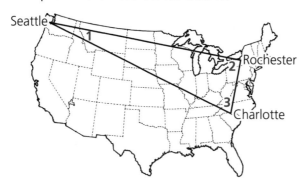

A triangle is formed by connecting the cities of Rochester, New York; Charlotte, North Carolina; and Seattle, Washington.

**Part A**

Name each type of angle formed.

∠1: _____ ∠2: _____ ∠3: _____

**Part B**

What is the measure of each angle?

∠1: _____ ° ∠2: _____ ° ∠3: _____ °

**Unit 7** Geometry, Part 1

**Read the problem. Write your answer for each part.**

**9** Use your protractor to help you solve this problem.

Look at ray *AB*.

**Part A**

On the figure above, draw ray *AC* to make an angle of 45°.

> *Ask Yourself*
> Where do I line up
> the protractor?

**Part B**

What is the vertex of the angle above? Explain how you know.

_____

_____

_____

_____

**Part C**

Is the angle you drew in Part A obtuse, acute, straight, or right?

*Answer:* _____

# Quadrilaterals

**Indicators** 5.G.4, 5 **CCSS** 5.G.3

✓ A **quadrilateral** is a polygon with 4 sides and 4 vertices. The figures below are all quadrilaterals.

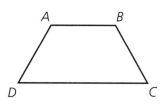

A **trapezoid** has 1 pair of opposite sides that are parallel; that is, always the same distance apart.

$$\overline{AB} \parallel \overline{DC}$$

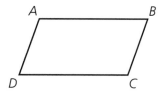

A **parallelogram** has 2 pairs of opposite sides that are parallel.

$$\overline{AB} \parallel \overline{DC} \qquad \overline{AD} \parallel \overline{BC}$$

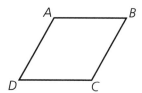

A **rhombus** has 4 sides of equal length and 2 pairs of congruent angles.

$$\overline{AB} \parallel \overline{DC} \qquad \overline{AD} \parallel \overline{BC}$$

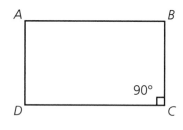

A **rectangle** is a parallelogram with sides that are perpendicular; that is, at 90° angles.

$$\overline{BC} \perp \overline{CD}$$

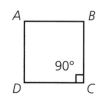

A **square** is a rectangle with equal sides.

$$AB = BC = CD = DA$$

✓ The sum of the interior angles of a quadrilateral is 360°.

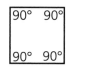

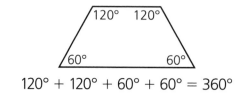

$$90° + 90° + 90° + 90° = 360° \qquad 120° + 120° + 60° + 60° = 360°$$

---

**Remember—**

**Parallel lines** are always the same distance apart. They never meet. The symbol ∥ means "is parallel to."

**Perpendicular lines** intersect at right angles. The symbol ⊥ means "is perpendicular to."

A **right angle** measures 90°.

An **acute angle** measures less than 90°.

An **obtuse angle** measures more than 90° but less than 180°.

All squares are rectangles and all rectangles are parallelograms. But **not** all parallelograms are rectangles and not **all** rectangles are squares.

**Read each problem. Circle the letter of the best answer.**

**1** A quadrilateral has 4 right angles. What kind of quadrilateral must it be?

   **A** square

   **B** rhombus

   **C** rectangle

   **D** trapezoid

> The correct answer is C. Only squares and rectangles have 4 right angles. So choices A or C could be correct. But the problem says nothing about the lengths of the sides. All squares are rectangles, so a rectangle covers all the possibilities.

**2** How do you know the figure shown here is a trapezoid?

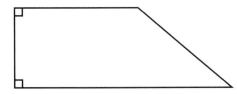

   **A** It has 4 sides.

   **B** It has 4 angles.

   **C** It has only 1 pair of parallel sides.

   **D** It has 2 pairs of perpendicular sides.

**3** What is the difference between a rectangle and a square?

   **A** All the angles of a square are 90°.

   **B** Two sides of a square are equal.

   **C** All the sides of a square are equal.

   **D** A square has two pairs of parallel sides.

**4** A quadrilateral has two pairs of parallel sides. What kind of quadrilateral must it be?

   **A** square

   **B** rectangle

   **C** rhombus

   **D** parallelogram

**5** If three angles of a quadrilateral total 280°, what is the measure of the fourth angle?

   **A** 20°

   **B** 40°

   **C** 60°

   **D** 80°

**6** Which statement about a parallelogram is **not** true?

   **A** It always has 4 sides.

   **B** It always has 4 angles.

   **C** It always has parallel sides.

   **D** It always has perpendicular sides.

**7** Look at the figure below.

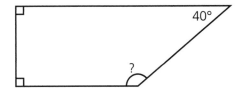

What is the measure of the missing angle?

   **A** 40°       **C** 140°

   **B** 90°       **D** 220°

**Read each problem. Write your answers.**

**8** Tyrone drew this floor plan of his bedroom.

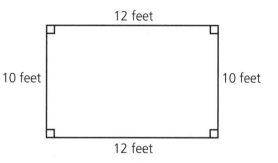

**Part A**

Classify the shape of Tyrone's bedroom.

*Answer:* _____ rectangle _____

**Part B**

Explain how you classified the shape of Tyrone's bedroom.

> Tyrone's bedroom is a rectangle. It is a parallelogram with sides that are perpendicular. The corners are right angles.

**9** In New York State, there are two major league baseball teams and many minor league teams. All the teams play on a baseball diamond, as shown by the diagram at the right.

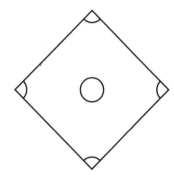

**Part A**

Which type of quadrilateral is a baseball diamond?

*Answer:* _____

**Part B**

Each of the angles of a baseball diamond is a right angle. What is the sum of the measure of all of the interior angles?

*Answer:* _____°

**Read the problem. Write your answer for each part.**

**10** A county park has the shape of a quadrilateral. Two opposite sides are parallel and 4 miles in length. The other two sides are also parallel, but they are only 2 miles in length. The adjacent sides are perpendicular.

**Part A**

Draw the park in the space below. Classify the shape of the park.

> **Ask Yourself**
> What do *parallel* and *perpendicular* mean?

*Answer:* _____

**Part B**

Explain why your classification is correct.

_____

_____

_____

_____

**Part C**

A trail goes from one corner of the park to the middle of an opposite long side, creating two shapes, a triangle and a quadrilateral. Classify the new quadrilateral formed. Explain why your classification is correct.

_____

_____

_____

_____

# Triangles

**Indicators 5.G.6, 7, 8**

✓ Triangles can be classified by the kinds of angles they have.

A **right triangle** has 1 right angle.

An **acute triangle** has 3 acute angles.

An **obtuse triangle** has 1 obtuse angle.

✓ Triangles can also be classified by the number of equal sides they have.

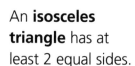

An **isosceles triangle** has at least 2 equal sides.

A **scalene triangle** has no equal sides.

An **equilateral triangle** has 3 equal sides.

✓ The sum of the measures of a triangle always equals 180°.

$m\angle A + m\angle B + m\angle C = 180°$

$50° + 60° + 70° = 180°$

✓ If you know two of the measures of a triangle, you can find the third measure.

First add the measures of the angles you know.

$45° + 75° = 120°$

Then subtract the sum of the two angles from 180°.

$180° - 120° = 60°$

The third angle is 60°.

### Remember—

A square corner symbol in a geometric figure means the angle measures 90°.

A right angle measures 90°.

An acute angle measures less than 90°.

An obtuse angle measures more than 90° but less than 180°.

The sum of the lengths of any two sides of a triangle must be greater than the length of the third side.

All three angles of an equilateral triangle have the same measure, 60°.

A triangle can be classified in more than one way. This is a right isosceles triangle. It has 1 right angle and 2 of its sides are the same length.

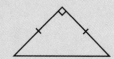

**Read each problem. Circle the letter of the best answer.**

**1** The sum of the measures of two angles in a triangle is 127°. What is the measure of the third angle?

A  45°

B  53°

C  180°

D  233°

The correct answer is B. The sum of the measures of a triangle is always 180°. So 180° − 127° = 53°.

**2** Why is the triangle shown below both a right triangle and a scalene triangle?

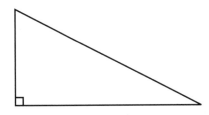

A  It has a right angle and no equal sides.

B  It has 2 acute angles and no equal sides.

C  It has an obtuse angle and 2 equal sides.

D  It has a right angle and 2 equal sides.

**3** Look at this isosceles triangle.

Which can this triangle also be classified as?

A  right

B  acute

C  obtuse

D  equilateral

**4** Which of these statements is true?

A  An isosceles triangle always has three equal sides.

B  A scalene triangle has no equal sides.

C  An acute triangle contains only two acute angles.

D  An obtuse triangle always has two obtuse angles.

**5** Which of these is an acute triangle?

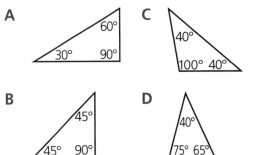

**6** What is the measure of the missing angle?

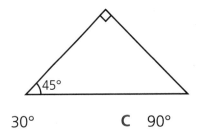

A  30°          C  90°

B  45°          D  180°

**7** A triangle has one obtuse angle. What must be true of the other two angles?

A  Their sum is less than 90°.

B  Their sum is more than 90°.

C  Each angle must be 90°.

D  One angle must be less than 90°, and one must be more than 90°.

**Read each problem. Write your answers.**

**8** Look at this triangle.

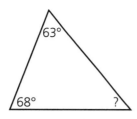

**Part A**

What is the measure of the missing angle?

**Show your work.**

$$68° + 63° = 131°$$
$$180° - 131° = 49°$$

**Answer:** _____49_____ °

**Part B**

What type of triangle is this? Explain how you know.

Two angle measures are given. Since the sum of the measures of a triangle is always 180°, add the two angles you know: 68° + 63° = 131°. Then subtract from 180°: 180° − 131° = 49°. This is an acute triangle, since all three angles are less than 90°.

**9** A pizza slice is triangular in shape.

**Part A**

How would this triangle be classified, according to the angles?

**Answer:** _____

**Part B**

How would this triangle be classified by sides?

**Answer:** _____

**Read the problem. Write your answer for each part.**

**10** The Jones family took a trip from their home in Albany to Plattsburgh. After seeing the sights for several days, they drove west to Binghamton. Then they drove home to Albany.

*Ask Yourself*
What kinds of angles does the triangle have? How many equal sides does it have?

**Part A**

If lines are drawn between their home and the cities they visited, what type of triangle is formed? Classify the triangle by angle and by length of sides.

Answer: _____ and _____

**Part B**

Explain your answer.

_____

_____

_____

**Part C**

If two angles of this triangle measure 35° and 40°, what is the measure of the third angle?

**Show your work.**

Answer: _____°

**Read each problem. Circle the letter of the best answer.**

**1** Which picture shows two perpendicular rays?

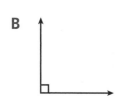

**2** What tool would you use to measure the angle of the roof on a drawing of a house?

**A** ruler

**C** protractor

**B** compass

**D** thermometer

Use this figure to answer questions 3 and 4.

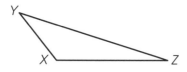

**3** What type of triangle is this?

**A** acute

**C** isosceles

**B** equilateral

**D** scalene

**4** Which two rays make up angle YXZ?

**A** $\overrightarrow{YX}$ and $\overrightarrow{XZ}$

**C** $\overrightarrow{XY}$ and $\overrightarrow{XZ}$

**B** $\overrightarrow{ZY}$ and $\overrightarrow{YX}$

**D** $\overrightarrow{YX}$ and $\overrightarrow{ZX}$

**5** A quadrilateral has two pairs of parallel sides. The sides are **not** equal in length. None of the angles measures 90°. What shape is the quadrilateral?

**A** trapezoid

**C** rectangle

**B** parallelogram

**D** rhombus

**6** What is the measure of the missing angle?

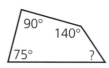

**A** 45°

**C** 55°

**B** 50°

**D** 60°

**7** Which word describes this angle?

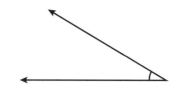

**A** acute

**C** straight

**B** obtuse

**D** right

**8** A triangle has two angles that sum to 90°. What must be true of the third angle?

**A** It must be a right angle.

**B** It must be an acute angle.

**C** It must be an obtuse angle.

**D** It must be a straight angle.

**Read each problem. Write your answers.**

**9** Joelle made a flat jewelry pin in art class. The shape of the pin has four equal sides. It has two acute angles and two obtuse angles.

*Part A*

Draw the shape of Joelle's pendant in the space at the right.

What is the name of this plane figure?

*Answer:* _____

*Part B*

Explain how you classified the shape.

_____

_____

_____

**10**  Use your ruler and protractor to help you solve this problem.

This trapezoid has been divided into three triangles.

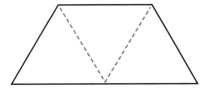

*Part A*

Classify the triangles formed by sides and angles.

*Answer:* _____ and _____

*Part B*

Explain how you know your answer is correct.

_____

_____

_____

**Read the problem. Write your answer for each part.**

11  ▦ ◠ Use your ruler and protractor to help you solve this problem.

### Part A

In the space below, draw two line segments of the same length, $\overline{AB}$ and $\overline{BC}$, that form angle ABC measuring 90°.

### Part B

Using the diagram drawn above, draw line segment AC to form triangle ABC. What are the measures of angles CAB and ACB?

*Answer:* _____° and _____°

### Part C

Explain how you found your answer to Part B.

_____

_____

_____

_____

# Unit 8
## Geometry, Part 2

As you work with shapes, you will learn more about their characteristics. The distance around a figure is its perimeter. You measure perimeter when you measure the distance around a soccer field. Suppose you need two pieces of paper that are exactly the same size. You need to have congruent figures. When you cut a piece of paper to make matching halves, you are cutting along a line of symmetry. This unit will help you understand more about geometry.

Lesson 1 **Perimeter** reviews how to find the perimeter of plane figures. You will also use the perimeter formula for rectangles.

Lesson 2 **Congruent Figures** reviews how to tell if two triangles are congruent. You will also review the relationship between corresponding parts of congruent triangles.

Lesson 3 **Similar Figures** reviews how to tell if two triangles are similar. You will find the ratio that compares the lengths of corresponding sides on similar triangles.

Lesson 4 **Symmetry** reviews how to draw a line of symmetry on a figure. You will also decide if a figure has more than one line of symmetry.

**Indicators** 5.G.1; 5.A.6

✓ The **perimeter** of a plane figure is the distance around it.

To find perimeter, add the lengths of the sides.

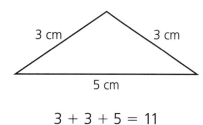

$$3 + 3 + 5 = 11$$

The perimeter of this triangle is 11 centimeters.

✓ If the figure is a rectangle, multiply the length by 2 and the width by 2, and then add the products together.

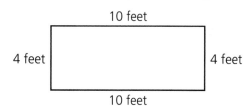

*Perimeter = 2 × length + 2 × width*
$$2 \times 10 + 2 \times 4 = 20 + 8 = 28$$

The perimeter of this rectangle is 28 feet.

---

*Remember—*

When finding perimeter, always give your answer in the units shown in the problem: inches, centimeters, etc.

To find the perimeter of a square, multiply the length of a side by 4, since all the sides are equal.

5 in.

5 in. ☐ 5 in.

5 in.

*Perimeter = 4 × length*
$$4 \times 5 \text{ in.} = 20 \text{ in.}$$

---

**Unit 8** Geometry, Part 2

**Read each problem. Circle the letter of the best answer.**

**1** Andrea is using the perimeter formula $P = 2l + 2w$. If $l$ is 9 feet and $w$ is 3 feet, what is the value of $P$?

**A** 12 feet

**B** 16 feet

**C** 24 feet

**D** 48 feet

> The correct answer is C. First substitute the values of the length and width in the formula: $P = 2(9) + 2(3)$. Then solve the equation: $P = 18 + 6 = 24$.

**2** What is the perimeter of a regular octagon with 2-inch sides?

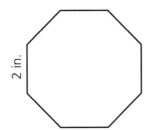

2 in.

**A** 2 inches          **C** 12 inches

**B** 8 inches          **D** 16 inches

**3** 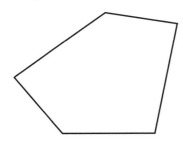 Use your centimeter ruler to help you solve this problem.

What is the perimeter of this figure?

**A** 10 cm          **C** 13 cm

**B** 12.5 cm        **D** 15.5 cm

**4** A square has a perimeter of 48 inches. What is the length of each side?

**A** 6 inches          **C** 18 inches

**B** 12 inches         **D** 24 inches

**5** Which of the following would give the perimeter of this rectangle?

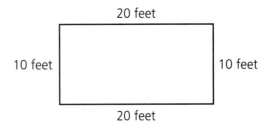

20 feet

10 feet          10 feet

20 feet

**A** $(2 \times 10) + (2 \times 20) = 60$ feet

**B** $(2 + 20) + (2 + 10) = 34$ feet

**C** $(2 + 10) \times (2 + 20) = 264$ feet

**D** $10 \times 20 = 200$ feet

**6** Allegany County, in western New York State, is a rectangle. It measures about 38 miles from north to south and 31 miles from east to west. What is the perimeter of Allegany County?

**A** 69 miles          **C** 138 miles

**B** 123 miles         **D** 146 miles

**7** Each square in the diagram below has a perimeter of 20 feet.

What is the perimeter of the shaded portion?

**A** 20 feet          **C** 60 feet

**B** 40 feet          **D** 80 feet

**Read each problem. Write your answers.**

**8** The South Street School has a fence completely around its square playground, except for an eight-foot opening.

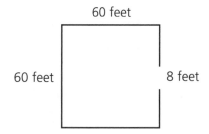

60 feet

60 feet          8 feet

*Part A*

How long is the fence?

*Answer:* _____232_____ feet

*Part B*

Explain how you found your answer.

> If the playground is a square, then all four sides are the same length. Multiply $4 \times 60 = 240$ feet. Next subtract the 8-foot opening: $240 - 8 = 232$. The fence is 232 feet long.

**9** Each square in the figure below has sides that are 4 feet long.

*Part A*

What is the perimeter of the whole figure?

*Answer:* _____ feet

*Part B*

Explain why your answer is correct.

_____

_____

_____

_____

**Unit 8** Geometry, Part 2

**Read the problem. Write your answer for each part.**

10  Use your inch ruler to help you solve this problem.

This diagram shows an award given to students with perfect attendance.

### Part A

Is the perimeter of the outside square greater than or less than 3 inches?

***Show your work.***

*Answer:* _____

### Part B

If the sides of the outside square are increased by 1 inch each, how would the perimeter change? Explain your answer.

_____

_____

_____

_____

Congruent figures have exactly the same shape and size.

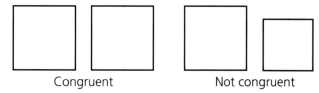

Congruent          Not congruent

Congruent figures do **not** need to be in the same position. You can turn or flip a figure and it will still be congruent.

These figures are all congruent.

Congruent figures are the same size. So the corresponding parts are the same.

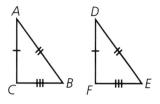

Corresponding sides are the same length.

$$\triangle ABC \cong \triangle DEF$$
$$AB = DE \quad BC = EF$$
$$CA = FD$$

Corresponding angles have the same measures.

$$m\angle A = m\angle D \quad m\angle B = m\angle E$$
$$m\angle C = m\angle F$$

## Remember—

The **corresponding parts** of congruent figures are the sides and angles that are in the same place on both figures.

The sum of the measures of a triangle always equals 180°.

The symbol $\cong$ means "is congruent to."

Tick marks across the sides of congruent figures mean those sides are equal. The sides with the same number of marks have the same length.

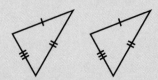

$m\angle A$ means "the measure of angle $A$."

**Unit 8** Geometry, Part 2

**Read each problem. Circle the letter of the best answer.**

**1** These two triangles are congruent. What are the measures of angles *B* and *C*?

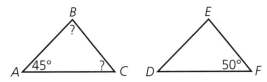

**A** 45° and 65°    **C** 75° and 45°

**B** 85° and 50°    **D** 45° and 50°

The correct answer is B. Congruent figures have exactly the same size and shape. So the corresponding parts are congruent: ∠*A* and ∠*D* = 45°, ∠*C* and ∠*F* = 50°, and m∠*B* = m∠*E*. The measures of ∠*B* and ∠*E* can be found by adding the two known angles and subtracting that sum from 180°: 45° + 50° = 95°, 180° − 95° = 85°. So ∠*B* and ∠*E* are both 85°.

**2** Which of these is a pair of congruent triangles?

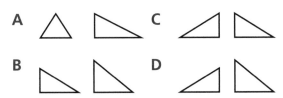

**3** In the diagram below, △*RST* is congruent to △*XYZ*.

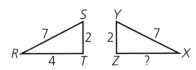

If *RT* = 4 cm, what is *XZ*?

**A** 2 cm    **C** 7 cm

**B** 4 cm    **D** 13 cm

**4** Look at these triangles.

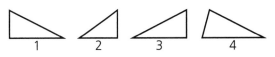

Which two triangles are congruent?

**A** 1 and 2    **C** 1 and 3

**B** 3 and 4    **D** 2 and 4

**5** The two triangles shown below are congruent.

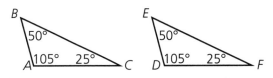

Which statement about the triangles is true?

**A** $\overline{AB} \cong \overline{DF}$    **C** ∠*C* ≅ ∠*D*

**B** ∠*A* ≅ ∠*E*    **D** $\overline{AC} \cong \overline{DF}$

**6** A large triangle has a perimeter of 11 yards. One side of the triangle measures 3 yards. If another congruent triangle had a second side 3 yards in length, which statement is true?

**A** The third side of the second triangle would measure 3 yards.

**B** The third side of the second triangle would measure 5 yards.

**C** The third side of the second triangle would measure 7 yards.

**D** The third side of the second triangle would measure 11 yards.

**Read each problem. Write your answers.**

**7** Look at these triangles.

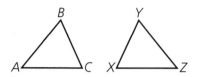

**Part A**

Are the triangles congruent?

*Answer:* _____yes_____

**Part B**

Explain how you know.

> Congruent figures are the same size and shape. Although the second figure is turned, it is still congruent to the first. The sides are the same lengths and the angles have the same measure.

**8** In the diagram at the right, △*ABD* is congruent to △*CDB*, m∠*BAD* = 60°, m∠*ABD* = 100°, and m∠*ADB* = 20°.

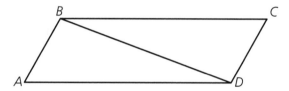

**Part A**

What are the measures of ∠*DCB*, ∠*CDB*, and ∠*CBD*?

**m∠*DCB* =** _____°

**m∠*CDB* =** _____°

**m∠*CBD* =** _____°

**Part B**

Explain how you found your answer.

_____

_____

_____

**Read the problem. Write your answer for each part.**

**9** Look at these triangles.

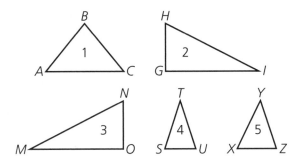

### Part A

Name two congruent triangles.

**Answer:** _____ and _____

### Part B

Name the corresponding sides.

**Answer:** _____ and _____

_____ and _____

_____ and _____

### Part C

Name the corresponding angles.

**Answer:** _____ and _____

_____ and _____

_____ and _____

*Ask Yourself*
Which triangles are exactly the same? Which are **not** the same?

# Similar Figures

**Indicators** 5.G.2, 3

✓ **Similar** triangles have the same shape, but they may be different sizes.

These triangles are similar **and** congruent.

These triangles are similar but **not** congruent.

These triangles are **not** similar and **not** congruent.

✓ The corresponding angles of two similar figures have the same measures. The corresponding sides of two similar figures have the same proportions.

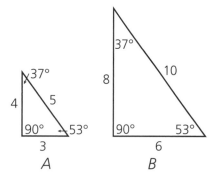

Each side of triangle *B* is twice as long as the corresponding side of triangle *A*. The corresponding sides have a ratio of 1 to 2.

Triangle *A*    $\dfrac{4}{8} = \dfrac{5}{10} = \dfrac{3}{6}$
Triangle *B*

## Remember—

**Congruent** figures have exactly the same shape **and** size.

All congruent figures are similar because they have the same shape. But not all similar figures are congruent, because they may or may not be the same size.

Figures do **not** have to be in the same position to be congruent or similar.

A protractor is a tool to measure the number of degrees in an angle. It can help you decide if two figures are similar.

A **ratio** is a comparison of two numbers.

**Read each problem. Circle the letter of the best answer.**

**1** Which triangles are similar?

**A** 2 and 3

**B** 3 and 4

**C** 1 and 2

**D** 1 and 3

> The correct answer is C. Triangles 1 and 2 are obtuse isosceles triangles. They are the same shape but different sizes. Triangle 3 is a right triangle, and triangle 4 is an acute isosceles triangle.

**2** Which statement about similar figures is true?

**A** Their angles are congruent.

**B** Their shapes are congruent.

**C** Their sides are congruent.

**D** Their angles are similar.

**3** What is the length of the missing side of triangle A?

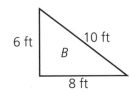

**A** 4 ft

**B** 5 ft

**C** 6 ft

**D** 7 ft

**4** These figures are similar.

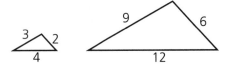

What is the ratio of the corresponding sides of the large triangle to the small triangle?

**A** 2 to 1        **C** 1 to 2

**B** 3 to 1        **D** 1 to 3

**5** These triangles are similar. What is the length of the side marked x?

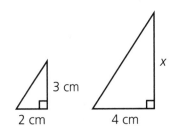

**A** 2 cm

**B** 3 cm

**C** 4 cm

**D** 6 cm

**6** Triangles *LMN* and *RST* are equilateral. The sides of △*LMN* are four times as long as the sides of △*RST*. The perimeter of △*LMN* is 36 yards. What is the length of one of the sides of △*RST*?

**A** 2 yards

**B** 3 yards

**C** 4 yards

**D** 6 yards

**Read each problem. Write your answers.**

**7** Look at the figures below.

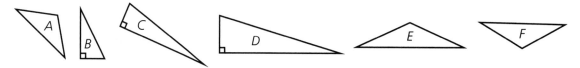

**Part A**

Which two pairs of triangles appear to be similar?

*Answer:* _____*C*_____ and _____*D*_____

_____*E*_____ and _____*F*_____

**Part B**

Explain why your answer is correct.

> Similar triangles have the same shape but are different sizes. Triangles *C* and *D* are similar right triangles. Triangles *E* and *F* are similar isosceles triangles.

**8** Use your ruler and protractor to help you solve this problem.

Look at the triangle at the right.

**Part A**

Draw a similar triangle with a ratio of 2 to 1.

**Part B**

If the angle shown in the first triangle is 30°, what should the corresponding angle in the triangle you drew measure? Why?

_____

_____

_____

**Read the problem. Write your answer for each part.**

**9**  Look at the two flags below.

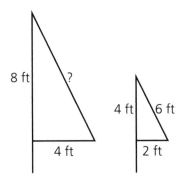

### Part A

What is the length of the missing measure in the first flag?

*Answer:* _____ feet

> **Ask Yourself**
> What are the corresponding sides?

### Part B

Explain how you found your answer.

_____

_____

_____

_____

### Part C

What is the ratio of the corresponding sides of the large triangle to the small triangle?

*Answer:* _____

✔ A figure is **symmetric** if it can be folded along a line to make halves that match exactly. A **line of symmetry** divides the figure into matching, or congruent, halves.

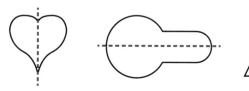

These figures are symmetric.

✔ Some figures have **more** than one line of symmetry.

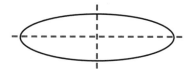 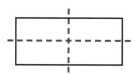

These figures have two lines of symmetry. They can be folded on **either** line to make matching halves.

*Remember—*

Some figures have **no** lines of symmetry.

A circle has an infinite number of lines of symmetry.

Sometimes a line of symmetry is **vertical,** or up and down.

Sometimes it is **horizontal,** or across.

A line of symmetry can also be **diagonal.**

**Unit 8** Geometry, Part 2

**Read each problem. Circle the letter of the best answer.**

**1** Which of the letters has no lines of symmetry?

R     T     U     V

**A** R

**B** T

**C** U

**D** V

> The correct answer is A. The letter R has no line of symmetry that can divide it into matching halves.

**2** Which of these pentagons shows a line of symmetry?

**A**   **C**

**B**   **D**

**3** How many of these figures have only one line of symmetry?

**A** one

**B** two

**C** three

**D** four

**4** Which of these has the most lines of symmetry?

**A**   **C**

**B**   **D**

**5** Which shape does **not** have a line of symmetry?

**A**   **C** (triangle)

**B** (square)  **D**

**6** How many lines of symmetry does this square have?

(square)

**A** one      **C** three

**B** two      **D** four

**7** Which statement about symmetry is **not** true?

**A** All figures have a line of symmetry.

**B** Lines of symmetry form congruent halves.

**C** Some figures have more than one line of symmetry.

**D** Symmetrical figures can be split into equal halves.

**Read each problem. Write your answers.**

**8** Look at this figure.

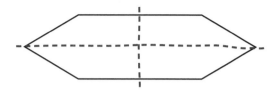

### Part A

How many lines of symmetry does the figure have?

*Answer:* _____ two _____

### Part B

Draw all the lines of symmetry on the figure above.

> A vertical line and a horizontal line are the only ways to split the figure into matching halves.

**9** Look at this stop sign.

### Part A

How many lines of symmetry does the shape of the stop sign have?

*Answer:* _____

### Part B

Explain your answer.

_____

_____

_____

_____

**Unit 8** Geometry, Part 2

**Read the problem. Write your answer for each part.**

**10** The picture shows the outline of the Empire State Building in New York City.

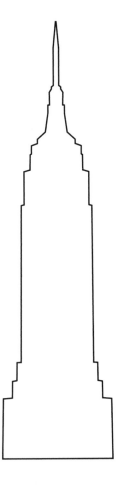

### Part A

Draw a line of symmetry through the Empire State Building.

### Part B

Explain why this is a line of symmetry.

_____

_____

### Part C

Is there more than one line of symmetry? Explain your answer.

_____

_____

_____

**Ask Yourself**
What will the figure on either side of the line of symmetry look like?

**Read each problem. Circle the letter of the best answer.**

**1** The triangles shown below are congruent. What is the length of the missing side?

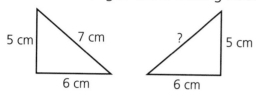

**A**  5 cm          **C**  7 cm

**B**  6 cm          **D**  18 cm

**2** If two triangles are similar, what is true about their angles?

**A**  They are always congruent.

**B**  They are never congruent.

**C**  They are always 90°.

**D**  They are never 90°.

**3** Which figure has no line of symmetry?

**A**      **C**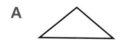

**B** 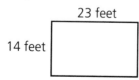     **D**

**4** Which of the following is the perimeter of this garden plot?

23 feet

14 feet

**A**  41 feet          **C**  322 feet

**B**  74 feet          **D**  400 feet

**5** The perimeter of a square room is 60 feet. Joanna wants to put a wallpaper border on all four walls of the room. She has put up the border on one wall. How many feet of border still need to be put up?

**A**  15 feet          **C**  45 feet

**B**  30 feet          **D**  60 feet

**6** Which pair of triangles is **not** congruent?

**A**

**B**

**C**

**D**

**7** The two rectangles shown below are similar. What is the length of the second rectangle?

9 in.          6 in.

12 in.          ?

**A**  6 inches          **C**  10 inches

**B**  8 inches          **D**  12 inches

**Read each problem. Write your answers.**

**8** Look at the figure at the right.

**Part A**

Draw all the lines of symmetry on the figure at the right.

**Part B**

Explain how you know your answer is correct.

_____

_____

_____

**9** Look at these triangles.

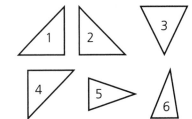

**Part A**

Name the triangles that are congruent.

**Answer:** _____

**Part B**

Explain how you know your answer is correct.

_____

_____

_____

**10** Each segment in the figure at the right has sides that are 6 feet long and 5 feet wide.

What is the perimeter of the entire figure?

*Show your work.*

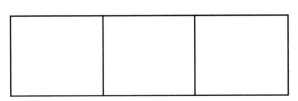

**Answer:** _____ feet

**Read the problem. Write your answer for each part.**

**11** Two triangles are similar. The first triangle has sides that measure 10 feet, 12 feet, and 16 feet. The ratio of the sides of the second triangle to the sides of the first is 1 to 2.

### Part A

What are the lengths of the sides of the second triangle?

Answer: _____ feet

_____ feet

_____ feet

### Part B

If the measure of one angle in the first triangle is 40°, what is the measure of the corresponding angle in the second triangle?

Answer: _____ °

Explain how you know your answer is correct.

_____

_____

_____

_____

# Unit 9
## Measurement

Measurement is one of the most common uses of mathematics. You use tools like rulers, scales, and even clocks to make measurements every day. Your physical education teacher measures the distance you run in class. Your father measures ingredients for a casserole. The doctor measures your weight and height. Sometimes it is not important to find an exact measurement. You can use personal references to estimate a measurement. This unit will help you understand measurement.

Lesson 1 **Customary Units of Length** reviews how to use an inch ruler to measure the length of objects. You will also change from small units of length to larger ones and from large units to smaller ones.

Lesson 2 **Metric Units of Length** reviews how to use a centimeter ruler to measure the length of objects. You will change from one metric unit to another.

Lesson 3 **Converting Measurements of Weight and Capacity** reviews how to find equivalent customary units of weight and capacity. You will also use a shortcut to find equivalent metric units.

Lesson 4 **Elapsed Time** reviews how to find how much time has passed using the start time and the end time of something. You will also find the start time and the end time when given the elapsed time.

Lesson 5 **Estimating Measurements** reviews how to use personal references to make estimates of measurements. You will also decide is an estimate is reasonable.

# Customary Units of Length

**Indicators** 5.M.1, 2 **CCSS** 5.MD.1

✓ **Inches, feet, yards,** and **miles** are customary units of length.

✓ You can use an inch ruler to measure length. It is marked with inches and fractions of an inch. On this ruler, each small space is $\frac{1}{8}$ inch.

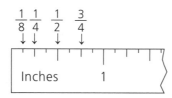

To read a ruler, line up one end of the object with 0 or the end of the ruler. Find the whole numbers the other end falls between. Then decide what fraction of an inch it is closest to.

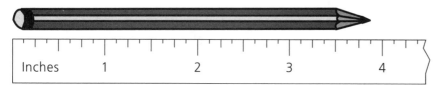

This pencil is $3\frac{7}{8}$ inches long.

✓ Sometimes you need to change one measurement unit into another unit. To change small units to larger ones, divide.

Semaj is 60 inches tall. How tall is he in feet?

There are 12 inches in 1 foot, so divide the number of inches by 12 to find the number of feet.

60 inches ÷ 12 = 5 feet

To change large units to smaller ones, multiply.

Semaj's father is 6 feet tall. How many inches tall is he?

1 foot equals 12 inches, so multiply the number of feet by 12 to find the number of inches.

6 feet × 12 = 72 inches

---

## Remember—

You can use equivalent fractions to read a ruler.

$$\frac{2}{8} = \frac{1}{4}$$

$$\frac{4}{8} = \frac{2}{4} = \frac{1}{2}$$

$$\frac{6}{8} = \frac{3}{4}$$

$$\frac{8}{8} = \frac{4}{4} = \frac{2}{2} = 1$$

Use the appropriate unit when you measure.

- Use inches for small things, like a pencil.
- Use feet for medium things, like a person or room.
- Use yards for longer things, like a playground.
- Use miles for the distance between things, like towns.

Abbreviations for customary units:

in. = inches
ft = feet
yd = yards
mi = miles

12 in. = 1 ft
36 in. = 1 yd
3 ft = 1 yd
5,280 ft = 1 mi
1,760 yd = 1 mi

---

**Unit 9** Measurement

**Read each problem. Circle the letter of the best answer.**

**1** Jenna bought 3 yards of fabric. What is this length in inches?

**A** 9 inches     **C** 36 inches

**B** 21 inches     **D** 108 inches

> The correct answer is D. First change yards to feet. There are 3 feet in a yard. So 3 × 3 feet = 9 feet. Then change feet to inches. There are 12 inches in a foot. So 12 × 9 = 108. There are 108 inches in 3 yards.

**2**  Use your inch ruler to help you solve this problem.

Dave found another insect that is 2 inches longer than the one shown. How long is Dave's insect?

**A** 4 inches     **C** 5 inches

**B** $4\frac{1}{4}$ inches     **D** $5\frac{1}{4}$ inches

**3** Use your inch ruler to help you solve this problem.

Xavier has some pieces of chalk of different sizes. The largest size is shown below.

The smallest piece of chalk is $\frac{1}{4}$ inch shorter than the largest one. How long is the shortest piece of chalk?

**A** $\frac{7}{8}$ inch     **C** $1\frac{1}{8}$ inches

**B** 1 inch     **D** $1\frac{1}{4}$ inches

**4** The label on a roll of wire says it contains 120 feet of wire. How many yards is that?

**A** 4     **C** 36

**B** 12     **D** 40

**5** Use your inch ruler to help you solve this problem.

What is the length of this line to the nearest $\frac{1}{8}$ inch?

**A** 1 inch     **C** $1\frac{3}{4}$ inches

**B** $1\frac{1}{2}$ inches     **D** $1\frac{7}{8}$ inches

**6** The distance from Chuck's News Stand to the bus stop is 180 inches. How many feet is that?

**A** 3 feet     **C** 45 feet

**B** 15 feet     **D** 90 feet

**7** Use your inch ruler to help you solve this problem.

Which of these nails is exactly $2\frac{3}{8}$ inches long?

**A**

**B**

**C**

**D**

**Read each problem. Write your answers.**

8   ⊞ Use your inch ruler to help you solve this problem.

Look at the moth below.

### Part A

To the nearest $\frac{1}{4}$ inch, what is the wing span of the moth shown above?

*Answer:* _____ $2\frac{1}{4}$ _____ inches

### Part B

Explain how you know your answer is correct.

> Line up the beginning of the inch ruler with the line at the left wing. Then read the whole numbers the moth falls between: 2 and 3 inches. It is $\frac{5}{16}$ more than 2 inches, so it is closest to $2\frac{1}{4}$ inches.

9    Andy measured the distance traveled by some turtles.

### Part A

Turtle 1 traveled 75 feet from where it was released and Turtle 2 traveled 28 yards. Which turtle traveled the greater distance?

*Answer:* _____

### Part B

Explain your answer.

_____

_____

_____

_____

**Read the problem. Write your answer for each part.**

**10** 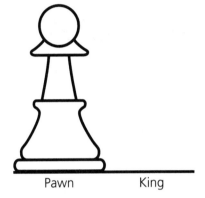 Use your inch ruler to help you solve this problem.

Brad likes to play chess. This game uses pieces of different shapes and sizes. One piece called a pawn is shown at right below.

**Part A**

How tall is the pawn, to the nearest $\frac{1}{8}$ inch?

> **Ask Yourself**
> What amount does each tick mark between the numbers stand for?

*Answer:* _____ inch(es)

**Part B**

Explain why your answer is correct.

_____

_____

_____

_____

Pawn          King

**Part C**

The object of the game is to capture a piece called the king. The king is $3\frac{5}{8}$ inches tall. Draw a vertical line to show the height of the king next to the pawn. Label it with the length. Explain why your answer is correct.

_____

_____

_____

_____

# Metric Units of Length

**Indicators   5.M.3, 4   CCSS   5.MD.1**

✔ **Millimeters, centimeters, meters,** and **kilometers** are metric units of length. A centimeter ruler measures length. It is marked with centimeters and millimeters. A millimeter is $\frac{1}{10}$ centimeter.

$1 \text{ mm} = \frac{1}{10} \text{ cm}$

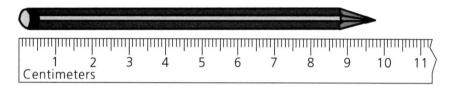

This pencil is exactly 98 millimeters long. To the nearest centimeter, it is 10 centimeters long.

✔ You can use a shortcut to multiply or divide to change one unit to another. To change small units to larger units, divide.

To change centimeters to meters, divide by 100 because there are 100 centimeters in 1 meter.

600 centimeters ÷ 100 = 6 meters

Or, use a shortcut. Move the decimal point to the left two places and cross off two zeros.

6̸0̸0̸ centimeters = 6 meters

To change large units to smaller units, multiply.

To change kilometers to meters, multiply by 1,000 because there are 1,000 meters in a kilometer.

8 kilometers × 1,000 = 8,000 meters

Or, use the shortcut. Move the decimal point to the right three places by adding three zeros.

8 kilometers = 8,000 meters

*Remember—*

Use the appropriate unit when you measure.

- Use millimeters for very small things, like a seed or a bug.
- Use centimeters for small things, like a pencil or a lamp.
- Use meters for longer things, like a car or a room.
- Use kilometers for the distance between things, like cities.

Abbreviations for metric units:

mm = millimeters
cm = centimeters
m = meters
km = kilometers

Metric units are multiples of 10:

10 mm = 1 cm
100 cm = 1 m
1,000 m = 1 km

**Unit 9** Measurement

**Read each problem. Circle the letter of the best answer.**

**1**  Use your centimeter ruler to help you solve this problem.

What is the length of this toy bus to the nearest centimeter?

**A** 4 cm      **C** 6 cm

**B** 5 cm      **D** 7 cm

> The correct answer is C. The exact measurement is $6\frac{2}{10}$ centimeters long. This is closest to 6 centimeters.

**2** Serena walked 550 meters to the bus stop. What is this distance in kilometers?

**A** 55 kilometers

**B** 5.5 kilometers

**C** 0.55 kilometer

**D** 0.055 kilometer

**3** Use your centimeter ruler to help you solve this problem.

Chris found this stone in his backyard. If he found another stone that was 3 cm longer than the stone shown, **about** how long was the second stone?

**A** 5 cm      **C** 7 cm

**B** 6 cm      **D** 8 cm

**4** The width of a desk measured 800 millimeters. How many centimeters wide is the desk?

**A** 8      **C** 80

**B** 10      **D** 100

**5** Grady has a ladder that is 200 centimeters tall. How could he change this height into meters?

**A** multiply 200 by 100

**B** divide 200 by 100

**C** add 100 to 200

**D** subtract 100 from 200

**6** Use your centimeter ruler to help you solve this problem.

Which ribbon is closest to 2 centimeters long?

A

B

C

D

**7** Antonio hiked 10.5 kilometers in Harriman State Park. How far did he hike?

**A** 1,500 meters

**B** 1,500 millimeters

**C** 10,500 centimeters

**D** 10,500 meters

**Read each problem. Write your answers.**

**8** 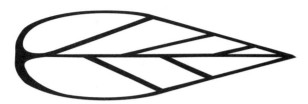 Use your centimeter ruler to help you solve this problem.

Look at the leaf below.

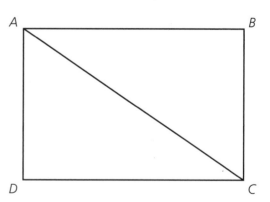

### Part A

Another leaf is double the length shown above. What is the length of the second leaf to the nearest centimeter?

*Answer:* _____16_____ centimeters

### Part B

What are the steps used to solve this problem?

> First measure the leaf. Its length is $7\frac{7}{10}$ centimeters, which is 8 centimeters when measured to the nearest centimeter. The word *double* is a clue to multiply by 2: $2 \times 8 = 16$. The second leaf is 16 centimeters long.

**9** Use your centimeter ruler to help you solve this problem.

Figure *ABCD* is a rectangle. Line segment *AC* is a diagonal.

### Part A

Measure the diagonal. To the nearest centimeter, what is its length?

*Answer:* _____ centimeters

### Part B

Explain how you found your answer.

_____

_____

_____

**Unit 9** Measurement

**Read the problem. Write your answer for each part.**

10 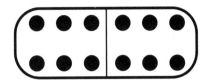 Use your centimeter ruler to help you solve this problem.

Dante measured this domino.

### Part A

If 15 of these dominoes were lined up, how long would they be from end to end?

*Answer:* _____ centimeters

### Part B

If 90 dominoes were lined up, how many meters would this be end to end?

*Answer:* _____ meters

> *Ask Yourself*
> How many centimeters are in a meter?

### Part C

Explain how you found your answer to Part B.

_____

_____

_____

_____

**Indicator 5.M.5  CCSS 5.MD.1**

✔ You can find equivalent units of weight and capacity by multiplying and dividing.

✔ To change a large unit to a smaller one, multiply.

Enrico bought 2 gallons of milk. How many quarts is that?

1 gallon = 4 quarts
$2 \times 4 = 8$ quarts

✔ To change a small unit to a larger one, divide.

Jenny put 48 ounces of meat in the freezer. How many pounds is that?

16 ounces = 1 pound
$48 \div 16 = 3$ pounds

✔ You can use a shortcut to change metric units. You can move the decimal point left or right.

To change milliliters to liters, divide by 1,000 because there are 1,000 milliliters in 1 liter.

6,000 milliliters $\div$ 1,000 = 6 liters

Or, use a shortcut. Move the decimal point to the left three places and cross off three zeros.

6,0̶0̶0̶ milliliters = 6 liters

To change kilograms to grams, multiply by 1,000 because there are 1,000 grams in a kilogram.

8 kilograms $\times$ 1,000 = 8,000 grams

Or, use the shortcut. Move the decimal point to the right three places by adding three zeros to the end of the number of kilograms.

8 kilograms = 8,**000** grams

**Remember—**

**Ounces (oz)** and **pounds (lb)** are customary units of weight.

16 oz = 1 lb

**Cups (c), pints (pt), quarts (qt),** and **gallons (gal)** are customary units of capacity.

2 c = 1 pt
2 pt = 1 qt
4 qt = 1 gal

**Grams (g)** and **kilograms (kg)** are metric units of mass.

1,000 g = 1 kg

**Milliliters (mL)** and **liters (L)** are metric units of capacity.

1,000 mL = 1 L

Unit 9 Measurement

**Read each problem. Circle the letter of the best answer.**

**1** Owen mixed a gallon of apple juice with a quart of grape juice to make a drink. How many pints of drink did Owen make?

   **A**  2

   **B**  4

   **C**  8

   **D**  10

> The correct answer is D. A gallon is equal to 4 quarts, so Owen made 5 quarts. A quart is equal to 2 pints, so multiply $2 \times 5 = 10$ to find an equivalent amount in pints.

**2** A can of peas has a mass of 400 grams. What is the mass of the can in kilograms?

   **A**  40 kg

   **B**  4.0 kg

   **C**  0.4 kg

   **D**  0.04 kg

**3** Kara bought 4 pounds of dog food. What is this weight in ounces?

   **A**  192 ounces

   **B**  96 ounces

   **C**  64 ounces

   **D**  36 ounces

**4** A pitcher holds 6 pints of liquid. What amount is this equivalent to?

   **A**  1 quart 2 pints

   **B**  3 quarts

   **C**  1 gallon

   **D**  1 gallon 1 pint

**5** A lion cub weighed 5.7 kilograms. What is the weight of the cub in grams?

   **A**  57 grams

   **B**  570 grams

   **C**  5,700 grams

   **D**  57,000 grams

**6** Mrs. Fields put a full gallon jug of apple cider on the table at the beginning of a meal. At the end of the meal, it contained only 1 quart. How much cider did the family drink during the meal?

   **A**  1 quart

   **B**  4 pints

   **C**  3 quarts

   **D**  8 pints

**7** The total amount of liquid in two measuring containers is 13,000 milliliters. How many liters is this?

   **A**  13

   **B**  130

   **C**  1,300

   **D**  13,000

**Read each problem. Write your answers.**

**8** A punch recipe calls for 1 pint of lemon juice, 3 pints of orange juice, and 2 quarts of ginger ale.

### Part A

How many gallons of punch does the recipe make?

*Answer:* _____1_____ gallon(s)

### Part B

Explain how you found your answer.

First combine the pints: 1 + 3 = 4 pints. Since 2 pints equal 1 quart, you can divide the number of pints to find the number of quarts: 4 ÷ 2 = 2 quarts. Then add the number of quarts: 2 + 2 = 4 quarts. This amount is equivalent to 1 gallon.

**9** Giant pandas are quite tiny at birth.

### Part A

If one baby panda weighs $\frac{1}{4}$ pound and a second panda weighs 5 ounces, which panda weighs more? Explain your answer.

_____

_____

_____

### Part B

An adult female panda weighs 180 pounds. How many ounces is that?

*Show your work.*

*Answer:* _____ ounces

**Read the problem. Write your answer for each part.**

**10** Each of the measuring cups holds 1 liter when full of liquid.

### Part A

How many total liters of liquid are in all three containers?

*Show your work.*

Answer: _____ liters

### Part B

How many milliliters is that?

Answer: _____ milliliters

**Ask Yourself**
How many milliliters
are in 1 liter?

### Part C

Explain how you found your answer to Part B.

_____

_____

_____

_____

# Elapsed Time

**Indicator   5.M.7**

✓ **Elapsed time** is the amount of time that passes from the start to the end of something.

If you know the start time and the elapsed time, you can find the end time by adding.

> A movie started at 7:00 and ended 2 hours 20 minutes later. What time did it end?

$$\begin{array}{r} 7{:}00 \\ +\,2{:}20 \\ \hline 9{:}20 \end{array}$$

The movie was over at 9:20.

If you know the end time and the elapsed time, you can find the start time by subtracting.

> Dinner ended at 6:45. If the Nagle family had been eating for 30 minutes, when did dinner begin?

$$\begin{array}{r} 6{:}45 \\ -\ \ {:}30 \\ \hline 6{:}15 \end{array}$$

Dinner began at 6:15.

If you know the start and end times, you can find the elapsed time.

> Stu's family left New York City at 9:15 A.M. They reached Allentown, Pennsylvania, at 11:45 A.M. How long did the trip take?

$$\begin{array}{r} 11{:}45 \\ -\ \ 9{:}15 \\ \hline 2{:}30 \end{array}$$

The trip took 2 hours 30 minutes.

### Remember—

These units of time are equivalent:

> 60 seconds = 1 minute
> 60 minutes = 1 hour
> 24 hours = 1 day

Multiply to find smaller units.

> 60 × 4 hours =
> 240 minutes

Divide to find larger units.

> 180 seconds ÷ 60 =
> 3 minutes

Regroup 1 hour as 60 minutes or 60 minutes as 1 hour.

$$\begin{array}{r} 6{:}15 \\ -\ \ {:}30 \\ \end{array} \quad \rightarrow \quad \begin{array}{r} 5{:}75 \\ -\ \ {:}30 \\ \hline 5{:}45 \end{array}$$

$$\begin{array}{r} 2{:}50 \\ +\,1{:}30 \\ \hline 3{:}80 \end{array} \quad \rightarrow \quad 4{:}20$$

A.M. times are between midnight and noon.

P.M. times are between noon and midnight.

**Unit 9** Measurement

**Read each problem. Circle the letter of the best answer.**

**1** Sophie started cleaning her room at 10:15 A.M. She worked for 40 minutes. Which clock shows the time she finished cleaning?

> The correct answer is C. To find the ending time, add the start time and the elapsed time: 10:15 + :40 = 10:55.

**2** A basketball game lasted $2\frac{1}{2}$ hours. It was over at 10:20 P.M. What time did the game start?

A   7:00 P.M.       C   8:00 P.M.

B   7:50 P.M.       D   8:50 P.M.

**3** Megan started washing her car at 4:45 and finished at 5:10. How long did it take her to wash her car?

A   15 minutes     C   35 minutes

B   25 minutes     D   45 minutes

**4** The Yankees–Mets game started at 1:15 P.M. It was over 2 hours 45 minutes later. What time was the game over?

A   3:25 P.M.

B   3:45 P.M.

C   4:00 P.M.

D   4:15 P.M.

**5** Mr. Cooper began cooking dinner at 3:55 P.M. He finished dinner at 6:25 P.M. How long did it take him to cook dinner?

A   1 hour 45 minutes

B   1 hour 55 minutes

C   2 hours 20 minutes

D   2 hours 30 minutes

**6** Miguel finished reading his book at 12:40 P.M. If he was reading for 1 hour 50 minutes, what time did he start reading?

A   10:40 A.M.      C   11:00 A.M.

B   10:50 A.M.      D   11:10 A.M.

**7** Ms. Johnson arrived at the library at 7:12 P.M. and left at 8:48 P.M. How long was Ms. Johnson at the library?

A   1 hour 36 minutes

B   1 hour 28 minutes

C   1 hour 42 minutes

D   1 hour 23 minutes

**Read each problem. Write your answers.**

**8** The Chung family drove from New York City to Albany. They left their house at 6:55 A.M. They arrived at 11:05 A.M.

How long did the Chung's trip take?

*Show your work.*

$$11:05 \longrightarrow 10:65$$
$$\underline{-\ 6:55} \qquad \underline{-\ 6:55}$$
$$\qquad\qquad\qquad 4:10$$

Answer: _____4_____ hours _____10_____ minutes

> Subtract starting time from ending time to find elapsed time. You can't subtract 55 minutes from 5 minutes, so regroup 1 hour as 60 minutes. The start time 11:05 becomes 10:65. Then subtract: 10:65 − 6:55 = 4:10. The Chung's trip took 4 hours 10 minutes.

**9** Len planned to write his book report in $2\frac{1}{2}$ hours.

**Part A**

The book report took him 40 minutes less than he planned. How many hours and minutes did the project take?

*Show your work.*

Answer: _____ hour(s) _____ minutes

**Part B**

Len finished the report at 2:45 P.M. What time did he start?

*Show your work.*

Answer: _____

**Read the problem. Write your answer for each part.**

**10** Angela is flying to visit her relatives in Atlanta. There are three flights from New York to Atlanta.

| Flight Number | Departure Time | Arrival Time |
|---|---|---|
| 368 | 7:45 A.M. | 9:50 A.M. |
| 712 | 10:45 A.M. | 1:00 P.M. |
| 964 | 2:19 P.M. | 4:38 P.M. |

*Part A*

Which flight takes the least amount of time?

*Show your work.*

**Ask Yourself**
How long is each flight? How do I calculate elapsed time?

Answer: _____

*Part B*

Angela decides to take Flight 964. It takes Angela 1 hour 10 minutes to drive to the airport. She must allow 45 minutes to check in. What time should Angela leave her house?

*Show your work.*

Answer: _____

# Estimating Measurements

To estimate measurements, you can use **personal references.**

| Customary Units of Comparison | |
|---|---|
| Inch | diameter of a quarter |
| Foot | length of a man's foot |
| Yard | height from floor to a doorknob |
| Mile | length of 14 football fields |

| Metric Units of Comparison | |
|---|---|
| Millimeter | thickness of a dime |
| Centimeter | width of your little finger |
| Meter | length of a baseball bat |
| Kilometer | the length of 9 football fields |

Liam estimated the width of his room as 6 feet. His foot is about 11 inches long. He took 9 steps. Is Liam's estimate reasonable?

$$\begin{array}{r} 11 \\ \underline{\times 9} \\ 99 \text{ inches} \end{array}$$

$$\begin{array}{r} 8\frac{1}{4} \text{ feet} \\ 12\overline{)99} \\ \underline{96} \\ 3 \end{array}$$

No, 6 feet is not a reasonable estimate of the width of Liam's room. It is closer to 8 feet.

**Remember—**

Use the appropriate customary unit when you measure.

- Use inches for small things, like a pencil.
- Use feet for medium things, like a person or room.
- Use yards for longer things, like a playground.
- Use miles for the distance between things, like towns.

Use the appropriate metric unit when you measure.

- Use millimeters for very small things, like a seed or a bug.
- Use centimeters for small things, like a pencil or a lamp.
- Use meters for longer things, like a car or a room.
- Use kilometers for the distance between things, like cities.

**Read each problem. Circle the letter of the best answer.**

**1** What unit of length would be used to measure the width of a paper clip?

**A** millimeters    **C** meters

**B** centimeters    **D** kilometers

> The correct answer is A. The width of a paper clip is very small. The best measure would be millimeters. The other units of length are too large.

**2** Greg estimated the soccer field is 100 feet long. Greg's walking pace measures about 3 feet. He walked the length of the soccer field in 20 paces. Is Greg's estimate reasonable?

**A** Yes, the answer should be **about** 3 × 30 = 90 feet.

**B** No, the answer should be **about** 3 × 20 = 60 feet.

**C** No, the answer should be **about** 3 × 50 = 150 feet.

**D** No, the answer should be **about** 3 × 90 = 270 feet.

**3** What is probably a good reference to measure 12 inches?

**A** a person's hand

**B** a person's foot

**C** a person's arm

**D** a person's leg

**4** Hilary knows a dollar bill is 6 inches long. If she used a bill to measure the width of a door, what would be a reasonable estimate of the width of a door?

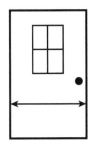

**A** 2 feet    **C** 5 feet

**B** $3\frac{1}{2}$ feet    **D** $6\frac{1}{2}$ feet

**5** What is a reasonable estimate of the length of a car?

**A** 5 feet

**B** 5 yards

**C** 50 feet

**D** 50 yards

**6** Tamara and her friends hiked for an hour. Which is a reasonable estimate of the distance they hiked?

**A** 4,000 inches    **C** 40 yards

**B** 400 feet    **D** 4 miles

**7** What is a reasonable estimate of the width of a parking space?

**A** 300 millimeters

**B** 30 centimeters

**C** 3 kilometers

**D** 3 meters

**Unit 9** Measurement

179

**Read each problem. Write your answers.**

**8** Deidre knows a baseball bat is about 1 meter long. She used a bat to measure the length of a swimming pool. She estimated the length of the pool to be 6 meters. Her brother John said it should be closer to 25 meters.

**Part A**

Which person's estimate is more reasonable?

**Answer:** _____John_____

**Part B**

Explain your answer.

> John's estimate is more reasonable. 6 meters is about 6 baseball bats long. That is much too small for the length of a swimming pool.

**9** Galen measured a plastic soda bottle using the width of his little finger.

**Part A**

If the soda bottle measured 16 finger-widths tall, **about** how tall is the soda bottle in centimeters?

**Answer:** _____ centimeters

**Part B**

Explain how you know your answer is correct.

_____

_____

_____

**Read the problem. Write your answer for each part.**

**10**  The track team ran 5 miles at practice yesterday.

*Part A*

***About*** how many football fields in length is that?

***Show your work.***

**Ask Yourself**
***About*** how many
football fields are
equal to a mile?

*Answer:* _____ football fields

*Part B*

Brent said he ran the length of about 28 football fields in 4 minutes.
Is this a reasonable estimate of the distance he ran?

*Answer:* _____

*Part C*

Explain your answer to Part B.

_____

_____

_____

**Read each problem. Circle the letter of the best answer.**

**1**  Use your inch ruler to help you solve this problem.

What is the length of this paper clip, to the nearest $\frac{1}{8}$ inch?

**A** $1\frac{1}{2}$ inches     **C** $1\frac{3}{4}$ inches

**B** $1\frac{5}{8}$ inches     **D** $1\frac{7}{8}$ inches

**2** A store is sold out of gallon containers of milk and has only quarts left. How many quarts must Teresa buy to equal 3 gallons?

**A** 4      **C** 12

**B** 8      **D** 16

**3** What would you do to convert yards to inches?

**A** divide by 36     **C** divide by 12

**B** multiply by 12   **D** multiply by 36

**4** Dennis started hiking on a trail at 8:10 A.M. He reached the end of the trail at 9:55 A.M. How long did the hike take?

**A** 45 minutes

**B** 1 hour 45 minutes

**C** 1 hour 55 minutes

**D** 2 hours 5 minutes

**5** Ben ran 1 mile, Jessica ran 5,400 feet, Lisa ran 1,800 yards, and Cliff ran $1\frac{1}{4}$ miles. Who ran the greatest distance?

**A** Ben      **C** Lisa

**B** Jessica  **D** Cliff

**6** The distance to exit 34 on the highway is 2.5 kilometers. How many meters is that?

**A** 25

**B** 250

**C** 2,500

**D** 25,000

**7** What is a reasonable estimate of the height of a house?

**A** 35 miles

**B** 35 feet

**C** 350 yards

**D** 350 inches

**8** Shelly cut a piece of rope to tie up a tomato plant. Which is a reasonable estimate of the length of the rope?

**A** 10 millimeters

**B** 10 centimeters

**C** 1 kilometer

**D** 1 meter

**Read each problem. Write your answers.**

**9** Curt is the tallest boy in his family.

**Part A**

Curt believes he is about 183 millimeters tall. Is this a reasonable estimate of his height?

*Answer:* _____

**Part B**

Explain your answer.

_____

_____

**10** A chef made 3 liters of French onion soup.

If a serving of soup is 250 milliliters, how many servings of soup did the chef make?

*Show your work.*

*Answer:* _____ servings

**11**  Use your centimeter ruler to help you solve this problem.

Maliki measured the bolt at the right.

**Part A**

To the nearest centimeter, what is the length of the bolt?

*Answer:* _____ centimeters

**Part B**

What would be the length in meters of 20 of these bolts laid end-to-end?

*Answer:* _____ meter(s)

**Read the problem. Write your answer for each part.**

**12**  The New York Philharmonic plays classical music in Lincoln Center in New York City.

### Part A

The orchestra started playing at 8:00 P.M. They took a 25-minute intermission and finished the concert at 10:15 P.M. How long did the orchestra actually play?

*Show your work.*

*Answer:* _____ hour(s) _____ minutes

### Part B

The audience is advised to arrive at the concert hall about a half hour before the performance begins. It takes the Thompson family 1 hour 40 minutes to drive from their home. What time should they leave for an 8:00 P.M. concert?

*Show your work.*

*Answer:* _____ P.M.

# Unit 10
## Statistics

Data is information. Newspapers, websites, magazines, and books display data in different types of graphs. Surveys and experiments are common ways of gathering data. You can use a table that shows the number of wins and losses for your favorite sports team to draw a conclusion about how well the team is playing. You can use a line graph that shows the daily temperature one week to predict the next day's temperature. This unit will help you understand statistics and data.

Lesson 1 **Data and Statistics** reviews good methods for gathering data and how to use a table. You will also find the mean of a data set.

Lesson 2 **Line Graphs** reviews how to make a line graph. You will also use a line graph to draw conclusions and make predictions.

# Data and Statistics

**Indicators** 4.S.1, 2; 5.S.1, 3

✓ **Data** is information, or number facts. You can collect data in many ways, such as experiments and surveys.

✓ A **table** is an organized list of data. The data is arranged in columns.

This table has three columns, showing the item, the size, and the cost.

**JUICE SPECIALS**

| Item | Size | Cost |
|------|------|------|
| Small | 8 oz | $1.25 |
| Medium | 12 oz | $1.45 |
| Large | 16 oz | $2.10 |

✓ You can use the data in a table to solve problems.

Which size has the lowest price per ounce?

To find the unit cost of each item, find its cost and its size. Then divide the cost by the number of ounces.

Small: $1.25 ÷ 8 = 0.156¢ per ounce

Medium: $1.45 ÷ 12 = 0.120¢ per ounce

Large: $2.10 ÷ 16 = 0.131¢ per ounce

The medium size juice has the lowest unit cost. It is *about* 12 cents per ounce.

✓ The **mean** of a set of data is the average. To find the mean, add all the values. Then divide by the number of values.

What is the mean price of the juice items?

$$1.25 + 1.45 + 2.10 = 4.80$$
$$4.80 ÷ 3 = 1.60$$

The mean price is $1.60.

---

*Remember—*

Each table consists of rows and columns.

**VACATION CHOICES**

| Group | City | Beach |
|-------|------|-------|
| Boys | 7 | 10 | ←Row |
| Girls | 6 | 9 |

↑
Column

A survey collects data from a **sample,** a small group that represents a much larger group. A **fair sample** is one that does not favor a certain answer.

"What is your favorite kind of music?"

Asking 100 people at a shopping mall would be a fair sample.

Asking 100 people at a jazz concert would *not* be a fair sample. The sample is more likely to answer "jazz."

The mean is sometimes called the *average*.

The mean is sometimes an actual data value in the set. Other times it is a number that is *not* one of the data values.

**Read each problem. Circle the letter of the best answer.**

**1** This table shows the areas of some states.

| State | Area (in square miles) |
|-------|------------------------|
| Idaho | 83,574 |
| Minnesota | 86,943 |
| New York | 54,474 |

Which of the following statements is true?

**A** The mean area is less than 70,000 square miles.

**B** The mean area is between 70,000 and 80,000 square miles.

**C** The mean area is between 80,000 and 90,000 square miles.

**D** The mean area is greater than 90,000 square miles.

> The correct answer is B. The mean is the average. To find it, first add all the values: $83,574 + 86,943 + 54,474 = 224,991$. Then divide: $224,991 \div 3 = 74,997$. This is between 70,000 and 80,000 square miles.

**2** Mr. Vasquez asked his students to name their favorite flavor of ice cream: V-Vanilla, C-Chocolate, S-Strawberry. The results are shown below.

C V V V C C S V
S C C V V V C S

Which table correctly shows this data?

**A**

| V | 8 |
|---|---|
| C | 5 |
| S | 3 |

**C**

| V | 6 |
|---|---|
| C | 4 |
| S | 6 |

**B**

| V | 7 |
|---|---|
| C | 6 |
| S | 3 |

**D**

| V | 7 |
|---|---|
| C | 3 |
| S | 6 |

**3** The attendance at four soccer games was 460, 886, 595, and 671. What was the average attendance at the games?

**A** 595  **C** 677

**B** 653  **D** 701

**4** Ella wants to find how many hours most students in her school spend on the Internet. What is the **best** group to survey?

**A** 50 members of the computer club

**B** 50 people at the mall

**C** 50 teachers in the school

**D** 50 students in the hallway

**5** Clark kept track of his spelling test scores.

75, 80, 95, 85, 65, 100, 95

What was Clark's mean score?

**A** 75  **C** 85

**B** 80  **D** 90

**6** A spinner has three sections labeled Red, Blue, and Green. Leilani spun the arrow 8 times, with the following results.

Red, Blue, Blue, Red,
Green, Green, Blue, Red

Which table correctly shows these results?

**A**

| Red | 3 |
|-----|---|
| Blue | 2 |
| Green | 3 |

**C**

| Red | 3 |
|-----|---|
| Blue | 3 |
| Green | 2 |

**B**

| Red | 2 |
|-----|---|
| Blue | 2 |
| Green | 3 |

**D**

| Red | 2 |
|-----|---|
| Blue | 3 |
| Green | 3 |

**Read each problem. Write your answers.**

**7** In 2010, tourists spent $46.2 billion in New York State. Visitors to California spent $95.1 billion, while visitors to Florida spent $62.7 billion.

What was the mean amount spent by tourists in the three states?

*Show your work.*

$$46.2 + 95.1 + 62.7 = 204$$
$$204 \div 3 = \$68$$

*Answer:* _____$68_____ billion

> To find the mean, first add all the amounts: $46.2 + 95.1 + 62.7 = 204$. Then divide by the number of states: 3. So $204 \div 3 = 68$.

**8** Ariel wants to know what is the most popular lunch at her school. She will ask people the question, "What is your favorite lunch in the cafeteria?"

*Part A*

Describe a fair sample that Ariel could use to find out the most popular lunch.

*Answer:* _____

*Part B*

Explain why your answer is a fair sample.

_____

_____

_____

_____

**Read the problem. Write your answer for each part.**

**9** The United States has many zoos. The San Diego Zoo has 4,000 animals, the Phoenix Zoo has 1,300 animals. The Bronx Zoo has 4,427 animals, and the Toledo Zoo has 4,723 animals.

*Part A*

Complete this table to show the number of animals in each of the zoos, from greatest to least.

| Zoo | Number of Animals |
|-----|-------------------|
|     |                   |
|     |                   |
|     |                   |
|     |                   |

*Ask Yourself*
Which zoo has the greatest number of animals? The least?

*Part B*

What is the mean number of animals in the zoos?

*Show your work.*

*Answer:* _____ animals

*Part C*

How much less is the mean than the number of animals at the largest zoo?

*Answer:* _____

**Indicators   5.S.2, 4**

✓ A **line graph** is a way to show change over time. Each point on the graph shows the data value for one moment in time, such as an hour, a day, or a week. A line connects the points.

Ashley recorded the daily high temperature in Millbrook, New York, one week in March.

**THIS WEEK'S HIGH TEMPERATURES IN MILLBROOK**

| Day | 1 | 2 | 3 | 4 | 5 | 6 | 7 |
|---|---|---|---|---|---|---|---|
| High Temperature | 46 | 40 | 43 | 46 | 53 | 56 | 54 |

She made this line graph to compare the data.

**HIGH AND LOW TEMPERATURES IN MILLBROOK**

On the side, Ashley wrote a **scale** in intervals of 5 degrees. Across the bottom, she wrote the time intervals, in this case, days.

Ashley plotted the points for the high temperatures and connected them with a solid line.

## Remember—

When a point falls *between* numbers on the scale, it stands for a number that comes between. You can estimate its value depending on how close it is to named numbers on the scale.

The scale on the bottom of a line graph tells the units of time. It is sometimes called a horizontal or *x*-axis.

The scale on the side of a line graph tells the units of measurement. It is sometimes called a vertical or *y*-axis.

The direction of a line on the graph shows the **trend** of the data. A line that goes upward means something is increasing over time. A line that goes downward means something is decreasing over time.

**Unit 10** Statistics

**Read each problem. Circle the letter of the best answer.**

Use this line graph to answer questions 1 and 2.

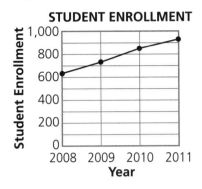

**1** What can you conclude from the graph?

  **A** The number of students is increasing by about 100 a year.

  **B** The number of students is increasing by about 50 a year.

  **C** The number of students is decreasing by about 100 a year.

  **D** The number of students is decreasing by about 50 a year.

> The correct answer is A. The student enrollment is increasing each year. There was an increase of 100 from 2008 to 2009. The increase was 125 from 2009 to 2010 and 75 from 2010 to 2011. So, the trend was an increase of about 100 each year.

**2** What is the **best** prediction for student enrollment in 2012?

  **A** 900

  **B** 975

  **C** 1,025

  **D** 2,000

**3** The table shows how the population of otters in a park has been changing over time.

| Year | 1 | 2 | 3 | 4 | 5 | 6 |
|------|---|---|---|---|---|---|
| Number of Otters | 80 | 70 | 40 | 50 | 50 | 60 |

Which line graph correctly shows this data?

**A**

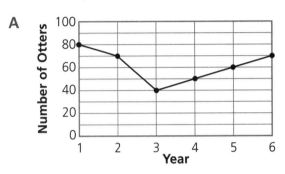

**B**

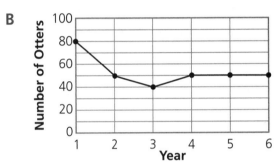

**C**

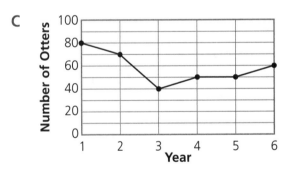

**D**

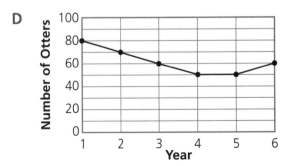

**Read each problem. Write your answers.**

**4** Aamir made a graph to show monthly rainfall in his town.

**Part A**

What conclusion can be drawn from the graph?

*Answer:* <u>Rainfall decreased by a half</u>

<u>                  inch each month.            </u>

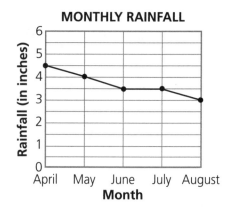

**Part B**

If the trend continues, how much rain would you expect to fall in September?

*Answer:* <u>   2.5   </u> inches

> Look at how the pattern changes from one month to the next: $4.5 - 4.0 = 0.5$, $4.0 - 3.5 = 0.5$, $3.5 - 3.5 = 0$, $3.5 - 3.0 = 0.5$. You can conclude that the rainfall decreases by 0.5 inch almost every month. From this you can predict that the rainfall will decrease 0.5 inch in September also: $3.0 - 0.5 = 2.5$.

**5** The table on the right shows the price of a one-way bus fare over several years.

**Part A**

Complete the graph to show the data from the table.

**Part B**

What can you conclude from the graph?

_____

_____

**BUS FARE**

| Year | Price Per Ride |
|------|----------------|
| 2007 | $0.85 |
| 2008 | $0.95 |
| 2009 | $1.05 |
| 2010 | $1.15 |
| 2011 | $1.25 |

**BUS FARE**

Price Per Ride

Year

**Read the problem. Write your answer for each part.**

**6** The table below shows the daily snowfall amounts in Syracuse over five days.

**JANUARY SNOWFALL**

| Date | Snowfall (in inches) |
|------|----------------------|
| 1/22 | 11.8 |
| 1/23 | 1.4 |
| 1/24 | 3.9 |
| 1/25 | 3.3 |
| 1/26 | 3.3 |

**JANUARY SNOWFALL**

Snowfall (in inches)

Date

**Part A**

Complete the graph above to show the data in the table.

**Part B**

Explain how you made your line graph.

_____

_____

_____

> *Ask Yourself*
> What is the greatest number that must be shown on the scale?

**Part C**

What conclusions can you draw about the rate of snowfall from January 22 to 26?

_____

_____

_____

# Statistics Review

**Read each problem. Circle the letter of the best answer.**

**1** A spinner has four sections labeled W, X, Y, Z. Carmen spun the arrow 10 times, with the following results.

Y, X, W, Y, Z, X, X, W, Y, X

Which table correctly shows these results?

**A**

| W | 4 |
|---|---|
| X | 3 |
| Y | 2 |
| Z | 1 |

**C**

| W | 2 |
|---|---|
| X | 4 |
| Y | 3 |
| Z | 1 |

**B**

| W | 2 |
|---|---|
| X | 4 |
| Y | 2 |
| Z | 2 |

**D**

| W | 1 |
|---|---|
| X | 2 |
| Y | 3 |
| Z | 4 |

**2** This table shows some of the longest rivers in the world.

**RIVER LENGTHS**

| River | Length (in miles) |
|---|---|
| Nile | 4,132 |
| Amazon | 4,200 |
| Missouri | 2,342 |
| Volga | 2,294 |

What is the mean length of the rivers?

**A** 3,225 miles

**B** 3,242 miles

**C** 4,300 miles

**D** 4,322 miles

Use the graph to answer questions 3 and 4.

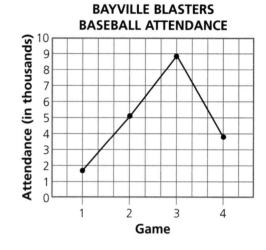

BAYVILLE BLASTERS
BASEBALL ATTENDANCE

**3** Which is the **best** prediction of the attendance for game 5?

**A** 1,000   **C** 6,000

**B** 4,000   **D** 9,000

**4** What is the mean attendance at games 1 through 4?

**A** 3,000   **C** 5,000

**B** 4,000   **D** 6,000

**5** Hans wants to find out what restaurants the students at his school like best. Which would be the **best** group for Hans to ask?

**A** 100 people at a pizza parlor

**B** 100 students in the cafeteria

**C** 100 children on the playground

**D** 100 people at a grocery store

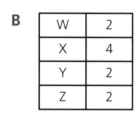

**Read each problem. Write your answers.**

**6** Faythe hiked some trails in a park this month. The table shows the length of each trail.

**TRAIL LENGTHS**

| Trail | Length (in miles) |
|---|---|
| Falls Trail | 2 |
| Rocky Trail | 9 |
| Lake Trail | 7 |
| Sunset Trail | 8 |
| Pine Trail | 4 |

**Part A**

What is the mean length of the trails Faythe hiked?

**Show your work.**

*Answer:* _____ miles

**Part B**

How much longer is Rocky Trail than the mean length?

*Answer:* _____ miles

**7** The graph shows temperatures at certain times on August 3.

**Part A**

What trend does the graph show?

_____

_____

_____

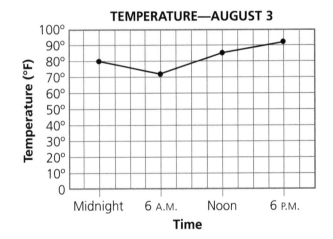

**Part B**

The temperature for noon on August 4 was expected to be 8° lower than the temperature at noon on August 3. What will the temperature be at noon on August 4?

**Show your work.**

*Answer:* _____ °F

**Read the problem. Write your answer for each part.**

**8** The population of New York City increased steadily in the 1800s.

NEW YORK CITY POPULATION

| Year | Population |
|------|-----------|
| 1840 | 312,701 |
| 1850 | 515,547 |
| 1860 | 813,669 |
| 1870 | 942,292 |
| 1880 | 1,206,299 |

POPULATION OF NEW YORK CITY

Population (in hundred thousands)

Year

**Part A**

On the grid above, complete the line graph to show how the population increased over time.

**Part B**

Explain how you made your graph.

_____

_____

_____

_____

**Part C**

What do you think the approximate population was in 1890?

*Answer:* _____

Unit 10 Statistics

**Read each problem. Circle the letter of the best answer.**

**1** A football team played 10 games. They sold 100,000 tickets for each game. How many tickets did they sell in all?

- **A** 1 million
- **B** 10 million
- **C** 1 billion
- **D** 10 billion

**2** There are three times as many oak trees as pine trees in a park. If $p = $ the number of pine trees, which expression gives the number of oak trees?

- **A** $3p$
- **B** $\frac{p}{3}$
- **C** $p + 3$
- **D** $p - 3$

**3** A computer copied a file in seven-hundredths of a second. What is seven-hundredths written as a decimal?

- **A** 0.0007
- **B** 0.007
- **C** 0.07
- **D** 0.7

**4** Which shape has the most lines of symmetry?

- **A** circle
- **B** square
- **C** regular hexagon
- **D** equilateral triangle

**5** The Empire State Building is about 0.38 kilometer tall. What is the equivalent of this height in meters?

- **A** 38 meters
- **B** 380 meters
- **C** 3,800 meters
- **D** 38,000 meters

**6** A quadrilateral has one pair of equal sides and one pair of unequal sides. Which statement describes this quadrilateral?

- **A** It is a square.
- **B** It is a trapezoid.
- **C** It is a rectangle that isn't a square.
- **D** It is a parallelogram that isn't a rectangle.

**7** Mr. Keeler made 15 hamburgers that each weighed $\frac{1}{4}$ pound. Their total weight was $\frac{15}{4}$ pounds. What is $\frac{15}{4}$ written as a mixed number?

- **A** $3\frac{1}{4}$
- **B** $3\frac{3}{4}$
- **C** $4\frac{1}{4}$
- **D** $4\frac{3}{4}$

**8** Mrs. Morris took 8 gallons of water on a camping trip. How many 1-quart bottles could she fill with this much water?

- **A** 4
- **B** 16
- **C** 32
- **D** 48

**Read each problem. Circle the letter of the best answer.**

**9** The estimated population of squirrels in a city park increases at a steady rate each year. Which line graph shows how the squirrel population changes?

A
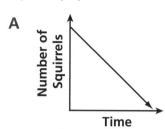

B
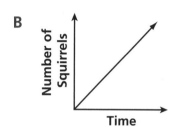

C
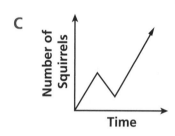

D

**10** If $x = 4$, what is the value of $6 + 3x$?

**A** 13          **C** 36

**B** 18          **D** 40

**11** What is the value of this expression?

$$5 + 2 \times 4 - (6 + 3)$$

**A** 4          **C** 19

**B** 10          **D** 25

**12** The table shows how long four students took to run the 50-yard dash.

**50-YARD DASH RESULTS**

| Student | Time (in seconds) |
|---------|-------------------|
| Javier  | 6.428 |
| Kevin   | 6.365 |
| Irene   | 6.406 |
| Tyler   | 6.38 |

Which list shows the students in order from least to greatest time?

**A** Tyler, Kevin, Javier, Irene

**B** Tyler, Kevin, Irene, Javier

**C** Kevin, Tyler, Javier, Irene

**D** Kevin, Tyler, Irene, Javier

**13** The flags shown below are shaped like similar triangles.

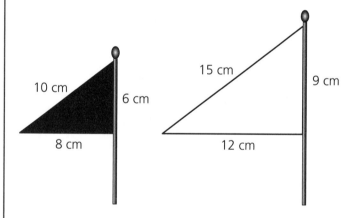

What is the ratio of the side lengths of the small flag to the side lengths of the large flag?

**A** 1:2          **C** 2:3

**B** 1:3          **D** 3:4

Practice Test

**Read each problem. Circle the letter of the best answer.**

**14** Marta ate $\frac{3}{5}$ of a pizza for lunch and $\frac{3}{8}$ of the pizza for dinner. Which statement correctly compares these two fractions?

A $\frac{3}{5} < \frac{3}{8}$

B $\frac{3}{5} > \frac{3}{8}$

C $\frac{3}{5} = \frac{3}{8}$

D $\frac{3}{5} + \frac{3}{8}$

**15** A canoe is 5 yards 2 feet long. What is this length in feet?

A   12 feet          C   16 feet

B   13 feet          D   17 feet

**16** Which of the following numbers is prime?

A   211          C   215

B   213          D   217

**17** Rachel left for the park at 4:13 P.M. She returned home 2 hours 54 minutes later. At what time did Rachel return home?

A   1:19 P.M.          C   6:57 P.M.

B   6:07 P.M.          D   7:07 P.M.

**18** Which list shows all the factors of 42?

A   0, 1, 2, 3, 6, 7, 21

B   1, 2, 6, 7, 21, 42, 84

C   0, 1, 2, 3, 6, 7, 14, 21, 42

D   1, 2, 3, 6, 7, 14, 21, 42

**19** In 2010, 999,845 people attended the Great New York State Fair. What is this number written in words?

A   nine ninety-nine, eight forty-five

B   nine hundred ninety-nine thousand, eight four five

C   nine hundred ninety-nine hundred, eight thousand forty-five

D   nine hundred ninety-nine thousand, eight hundred forty-five

**20** What is the value of $\frac{b \times 8}{2}$ when $b = 4$?

A   6          C   16

B   8          D   24

**21** In the diagram below, triangle *WXZ* is congruent to triangle *YZX*.

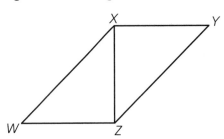

Which line segment must have the same length as $\overline{WZ}$?

A   $\overline{WX}$          C   $\overline{XZ}$

B   $\overline{YX}$          D   $\overline{YZ}$

**22** Which of the following is correct?

A   1.06 = 1.60          C   1.84 > 1.90

B   1.47 > 1.39          D   1.14 < 1.06

**Read each problem. Circle the letter of the best answer.**

**23** The snow in Andrew's yard has been melting for a week. The graph shows how the depth of the snow is decreasing.

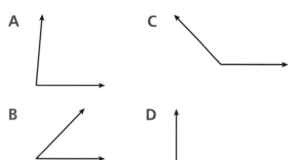

**DEPTH OF MELTING SNOW**

If the snow continues to melt at the same rate, how deep will it be on day 10?

A   0 centimeter

B   4 centimeters

C   8 centimeters

D   12 centimeters

**24** Which of the following angles is obtuse?

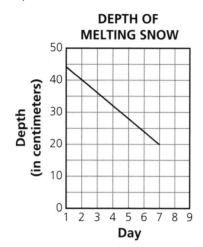

A

C

B

D

**25** The Adirondack Park area is approximately 24,281 square kilometers. What is this number rounded to the nearest thousand?

A   24,000          C   24,300

B   24,200          D   25,000

**26** The picture shows a fifth-grade student watering a plant.

Which is the **best** estimate of the height of the plant?

A   1 meter          C   1 millimeter

B   1 kilometer      D   1 centimeter

**27** Which of the following shows a pair of similar triangles?

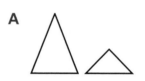

A

B

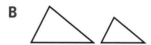

C

D

**28** Three hives of bees produced 6.18, 4.95, and 6.87 pounds of honey. Which is the **best** estimate of the total amount of honey produced?

A   16 pounds          C   18 pounds

B   17 pounds          D   19 pounds

Practice Test

**Read each problem. Circle the letter of the best answer.**

**29** The diagram shows a bicycle trail around the border of a park. The length of each section is marked in kilometers.

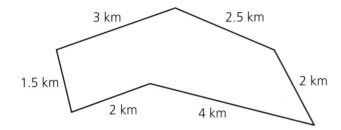

What is the perimeter of the park?

**A** 12 kilometers    **C** 14 kilometers

**B** 13 kilometers    **D** 15 kilometers

**30** In six soccer games, Sam's team scored 3, 0, 4, 5, 4, and 2 goals. What was the mean number of goals they scored per game?

**A** 2    **C** 4

**B** 3    **D** 5

**31** At a summer camp, there were 12 campers from Syracuse and 8 campers from Utica. What was the ratio of the number of campers from Syracuse to the number from Utica?

**A** 2:1    **C** 3:2

**B** 3:1    **D** 4:3

**32** Which two lines appear to be perpendicular?

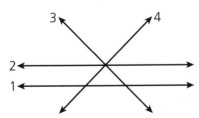

**A** 1 and 2    **C** 2 and 4

**B** 1 and 3    **D** 3 and 4

**33** The table shows recent data on the populations of four cities.

**CITY POPULATION**

| City | Population |
|------|-----------|
| New York City | 8,175,133 |
| Chicago | 2,695,598 |
| Houston | 2,099,451 |
| Los Angeles | 3,792,261 |

Which list shows these cities in order from greatest to least population?

**A** New York City, Chicago, Houston, Los Angeles

**B** New York City, Chicago, Los Angeles, Houston

**C** New York City, Los Angeles, Houston, Chicago

**D** New York City, Los Angeles, Chicago, Houston

**34** Tracy cut three 15-centimeter pieces of straw. She connected their ends together to make a triangle. Which describes the triangle Tracy made?

**A** equilateral    **C** scalene

**B** isosceles    **D** right

**35** A basketball court is shaped like a rectangle with a length of 80 feet and a width of 50 feet. What is the perimeter of this basketball court?

**A** 130 feet    **C** 4,000 feet

**B** 260 feet    **D** 8,000 feet

**Read each problem. Circle the letter of the best answer.**

**36** Nate asked 50 people what place in New York City they like the best. Twenty-two people said the Central Park. Sixteen people said Ellis Island, and 11 people said Coney Island. Which table shows this data?

**A**

| NYC Spot | Number |
|---|---|
| Central Park | 22 |
| Ellis Island | 16 |
| Coney Island | 11 |

**B**

| NYC Spot | Number |
|---|---|
| Central Park | 16 |
| Ellis Island | 22 |
| Coney Island | 11 |

**C**

| NYC Spot | Number |
|---|---|
| Central Park | 22 |
| Ellis Island | 11 |
| Coney Island | 16 |

**D**

| NYC Spot | Number |
|---|---|
| Central Park | 50 |
| Ellis Island | 16 |
| Coney Island | 22 |

**37** In triangle $PQR$, m$\angle P = 100°$ and m$\angle Q = 60°$.

What is the measure of $\angle R$?

**A** 20°       **C** 40°

**B** 30°       **D** 80°

**38** Pedro ate $\frac{3}{12}$ of a pie. His brother ate $\frac{2}{12}$ of the pie. What fraction of the pie did they eat in all?

**A** $\frac{1}{12}$       **C** $\frac{5}{12}$

**B** $\frac{5}{24}$       **D** $\frac{6}{144}$

**39** Use your inch ruler to help you solve this problem.

To the nearest $\frac{1}{4}$ inch, what is the length of this piece of yarn?

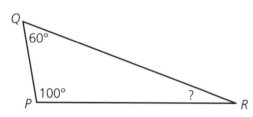

**A** 4 inches       **C** $3\frac{1}{2}$ inches

**B** $3\frac{3}{4}$ inches       **D** $3\frac{1}{4}$ inches

**40** There are 24 students in Mateo's class. Twenty of the students went on a field trip to Lake George. What fraction (in lowest terms) of the class went on the field trip?

**A** $\frac{3}{4}$       **C** $\frac{5}{6}$

**B** $\frac{4}{5}$       **D** $\frac{7}{8}$

**41** Carly's pencil is $7\frac{1}{8}$ inches long. Lara's pencil is $5\frac{3}{8}$ inches long. How much longer is Carly's pencil than Lara's pencil?

**A** $1\frac{2}{8}$ inches       **C** $2\frac{2}{8}$ inches

**B** $1\frac{6}{8}$ inches       **D** $2\frac{6}{8}$ inches

Practice Test

**Read each problem. Write your answers.**

**42** An elm tree is 48 years older than the house next to it. The elm tree is 225 years old. The equation $n + 48 = 225$ can be solved to find $n$, the age of the house in years.

Solve the equation $n + 48 = 225$ for $n$.

**Show your work.**

$n =$ _____ years

**43** A train is carrying a shipment of 170 motorcycles. Each motorcycle weighs 435 pounds. What is the total weight of this shipment of motorcycles?

**Show your work.**

*Answer:* _____ pounds

**Read the problem. Write your answer for each part.**

**44** There are 500 seals on an island, and 35% of them are pups.

***Part A***

What is 35% written as a decimal?

***Answer:*** ____________

***Part B***

What is 35% written as a fraction in lowest terms?

***Show your work.***

***Answer:*** ____________

***Part C***

How many of the seals on the island are pups?

***Show your work.***

***Answer:*** ____________ pups

**Read the problem. Write your answer for each part.**

**45** Becca leads tours of Niagara Falls. The table shows how many people she led on tours on six days in May.

**PEOPLE ON BECCA'S TOURS**

| Date | Number of People |
|------|------------------|
| May 1 | 110 |
| May 2 | 130 |
| May 3 | 150 |
| May 4 | 170 |
| May 5 | 190 |
| May 6 | 210 |

*Part A*

On the grid below, make a line graph to show this data.

Be sure to
- title the graph
- label the axes
- graph all the data
- provide the graph with a scale

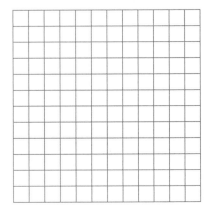

*Part B*

If the pattern continues, how many people will she lead on May 20th?

*Show your work.*

*Answer:* _____ people

**Read each problem. Write your answers.**

**46** The diagram shows the path of an airplane after takeoff.

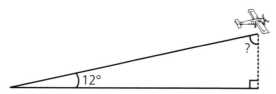

What is the measure of the angle marked with a question mark?

*Show your work.*

*Answer:* _____ °

**47** Jeffrey wrote this number pattern on the board.

3, 5, 7, 9, …

*Part A*

What would be the 5th number in this pattern?

*Answer:* _____

*Part B*

Explain how you can find the 100th number in the pattern.

_____

_____

_____

_____

**Read the problem. Write your answer for each part.**

**48** Use your ruler and protractor to help you solve this problem.

### Part A

In the space below, draw triangle *ABC* so that angle *A* measures 80°
and angle *C* measures 40°.

### Part B

What is the measure of angle *B*?

*Answer:* _____°

### Part C

Sarah wanted to draw a triangle with two 100° angles. Explain how
you know a triangle cannot have two 100° angles.

_____

_____

_____

_____

**Read the problem. Write your answer for each part.**

**49** These square tiles measure 9 inches on each side.

9 in.    9 in.    9 in.    9 in.

9 in.    9 in.    9 in.    9 in.

### Part A

What is the perimeter of each tile?

**Show your work.**

Answer: _____ inches

### Part B

Niva put these four tiles together to make a larger square. What was the perimeter of the larger square she made?

Answer: _____ inches

Explain how you found your answer.

_____

_____

_____

_____

# Glossary

## A

| | |
|---|---|
| **acute angle** | an angle that measures less than 90° |
| **acute triangle** | a triangle with three acute angles |
| **algebraic expression** | an expression that contains symbols, or letters, numbers, and operations |
| **angle** | a figure formed by two rays that share an endpoint and extend in different directions |
| **associative property** | allows grouping of numbers with parentheses to be added or multiplied: $a + (b + c) = (a + b) + c$; $a \times (b \times c) = (a \times b) \times c$ |

## C

| | |
|---|---|
| **centimeter** | a unit of length in the metric system; used to measure short lengths |
| **common denominator** | a number that is a multiple of every denominator of the fractions in a set |
| **common factor** | a factor that two or more whole numbers share |
| **common multiple** | a multiple that two or more whole numbers share |
| **commutative property** | allows numbers to be added or multiplied in any order: $a + b = b + a$; $a \times b = b \times a$ |
| **compare** | to decide which of two numbers is greater in value |
| **composite number** | a whole number that has more than two factors |
| **congruent** | equal in length, measure, or shape |
| **constant** | a number that does not change |
| **corresponding parts** | sides and angles that are in the same place on congruent and similar figures |
| **cup** | a unit of capacity in the customary system |

# D

**data**      information in the form of numbers

**decimal**      a number with values in places to the right of the decimal point

**degree**      a unit of angle measure

**denominator**      the number of parts in the whole or set, the number on the bottom of a fraction

**diagonal**      slanted

**dividend**      the number being divided in a division problem

**divisible**      able to be divided by

**divisor**      the number doing the dividing in a division problem

# E

**elapsed time**      the amount of time that passes from the start of something until the end

**equation**      a mathematical statement that shows two expressions are equal

**equilateral triangle**      a triangle with three sides of the same length and three 60° angles

**equivalent**      equal

**equivalent fractions**      two or more fractions that represent the same value

**estimation**      a way to find a value that is close but not exact

**evaluate**      to find the value of an expression

**expanded form**      a way to write a number in which each digit is expressed as the product of its face value and a power of ten

**expression**      a grouping of numbers, symbols, and operations that show the value of something

# F

**factors**     whole numbers that multiply to form a product

**fair sample**     a sample that does not favor a certain answer

**foot**     a medium unit of length in the customary system

**fraction**     part of a whole

# G

**gallon**     a large unit of capacity in the customary system

**gram**     a small unit of mass in the metric system

**greatest common factor**     the largest of the common factors between two or more numbers

# H

**higher terms**     when the terms of an equivalent fraction are greater than the original fraction

**horizontal**     across

# I

**improper fraction**     a fraction in which the numerator is equal to or greater than the denominator

**inch**     a small unit of length in the customary system

**intersecting lines**     lines that meet at a point

**inverse operations**     operations that undo each other, opposite operations. Addition and subtraction are inverse operations. Multiplication and division are inverse operations.

**isolate**     to get a variable by itself on one side of an equation

**isosceles triangle**     a triangle with at least two equal sides

# K

**kilogram**       a large unit of mass in the metric system

**kilometer**      a unit of distance in the metric system

# L

**least common multiple**       the smallest of the common multiples between two or more numbers

**line**       a figure made up of points that extends forever in both directions

**line graph**       a data display that shows change over time

**line of symmetry**       a line that can be drawn through a figure to divide it into congruent halves

**line segment**       a figure made up of points with two endpoints

**liter**       a unit of capacity in the metric system

**lowest terms**       when the terms of a fraction cannot be divided by a number other than one; simplest form

# M

**mean**       the sum of the data values divided by the number of values; the average

**meter**       a medium unit of length in the metric system

**mile**       a unit of distance in the customary system

**milliliter**       a small unit of capacity in the metric system

**millimeter**       a small unit of length in the metric system

**mixed number**       a whole number plus a fraction

**multiple**       the product of a number and a nonzero whole number

# N

**number line**    a line showing numbers in order from least to greatest

**numerator**    the number of parts talked about, the number on the top of a fraction

# O

**obtuse angle**    an angle the measures more than 90° but less than 180°

**obtuse triangle**    a triangle with one obtuse angle

**order**    to arrange numbers by value from least to greatest or from greatest to least

**order of operations**    the order in which operations are performed in a multi-operation expression: parentheses, multiplication and division from left to right, addition and subtraction from left to right

**ounce**    a small unit of weight in the customary system

# P

**parallel lines**    lines that are always the same distance apart and never touch

**parallelogram**    a quadrilateral with two pairs of parallel sides

**parentheses**    grouping symbols ( ) that indicate an operation should be done first

**pattern**    a sequence or design that repeats or grows according to a rule

**percent**    a ratio that compares a number to 100, written with the symbol %

**perimeter**    the distance around a figure

**perpendicular lines**    lines that meet at a right angle

**personal references**    everyday things that help you estimate measurements

**pint**    a small unit of capacity in the customary system

**place value**    the value given to the place a digit has in a number; each place has a value 10 times greater than the place to its right

| MILLIONS | HUNDRED THOUSANDS | TEN THOUSANDS | THOUSANDS | HUNDREDS | TENS | ONES |
|---|---|---|---|---|---|---|
| 7, | 6 | 5 | 4, | 3 | 2 | 1 |

**pound**    a unit of weight in the capacity system

**prime number**    a whole number that has exactly two factors, 1 and itself

**product**    the answer in a multiplication problem

**protractor**    a tool used to measure the size of an angle

# Q

**quadrilateral**    a polygon with four sides

**quart**    a unit of capacity in the customary system

**quotient**    the answer in a division problem

# R

**ratio**    a comparison of two numbers

**ray**    a figure that has one endpoint and extends forever in the other direction

**rectangle**    a parallelogram with four right angles

**remainder**    the number left when the dividend cannot be divided evenly

**rhombus**    a parallelogram with four equal sides

**right angle**    an angle that measures 90°

**right triangle**    a triangle with one right angle

**round**    to replace a number with a close number that tells about how many or how much

**rule**    a description of how a pattern changes

# S

**sample**    a small group that represents a much larger group

**scale**    the numbers along the side and bottom of a graph that give the units of time and measurement

**scalene triangle**    a triangle with no equal sides

**similar**    describes two figures that are the same shape but can be different sizes

**square**    a rectangle with four equal sides

**standard form**    a number written as the sum of the values of its places

**straight angle**    an angle that measures exactly 180°; forms a straight line

**symmetric**    able to be divided into matching halves

# T

**table**    a data display with rows and columns

**terms**    the numerator and denominator of a fraction

**trapezoid**    a quadrilateral with exactly one pair of parallel sides

**trend**    the direction of a set of data

# V

**variable**    a symbol or letter that stands for a value that is unknown or can change

**vertex**    the endpoint shared by the two rays that form an angle; the point where lines, line segments, or rays meet

**vertical**    up and down

# W

**word form**            a number name written in words

# Y

**yard**            a medium unit of length in the customary system

<

>

≅

≈

∥

⊥

← 5/8

← 5/8

is greater than
symbol

is less than
symbol

is approximately
equal to symbol

is congruent to
symbol

is perpendicular to
symbol

is parallel to
symbol

denominator

numerator

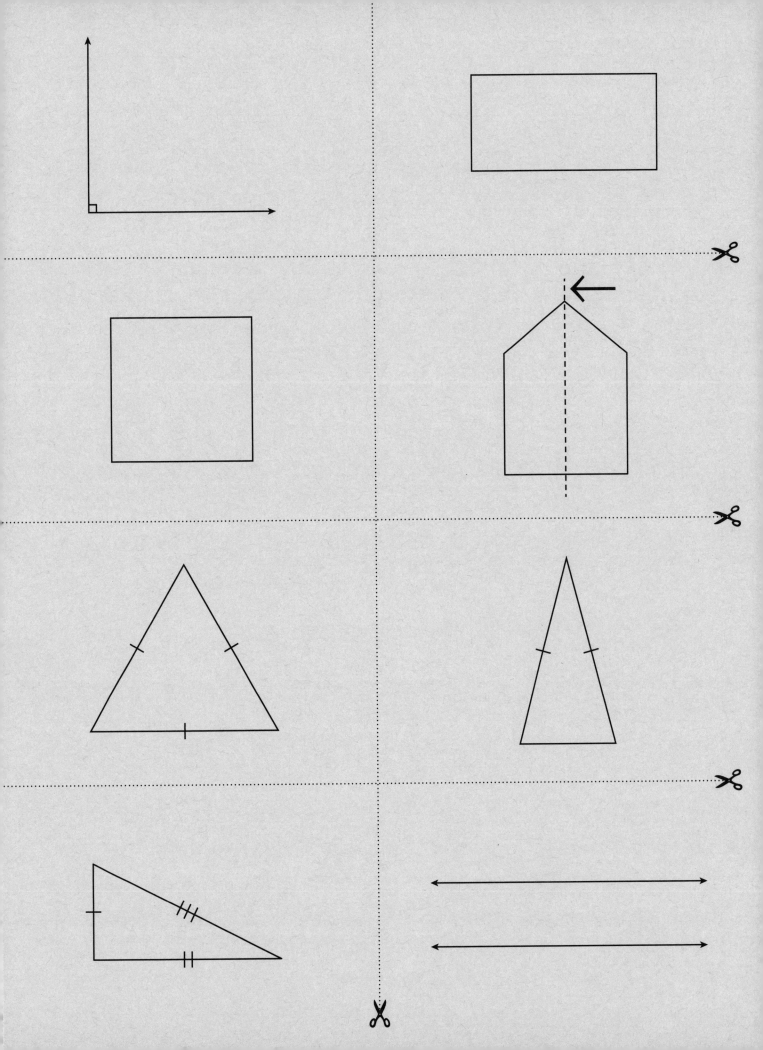

| | |
|---|---|
| rectangle | right angle |
| line of symmetry | square |
| isosceles triangle | equilateral triangle |
| parallel lines | scalene triangle |